TAKING STOCK

Advance Praise for
Taking Stock

"In *Taking Stock*, I enjoyed experiencing the journey of a great American leader. Peter de Silva shares his ups and downs and persistence to succeed. Peter's journey has been heroic."
—**Terry Dunn**, former president and CEO, JE Dunn Construction; former chair, Federal Reserve Bank of Kansas City

"At TD Ameritrade, Peter was a valuable expert in the wealth management and marketing realms. His real strength, however, was his influence on his peers and the impact he had throughout his entire organization. His people knew that Peter cared about them, and they would have followed him anywhere. It was not an accident that we were the best in the world at what we did."
—**Joe Moglia**, former board chair, TD Ameritrade; chair of Athletics and executive director, football program, Coastal Carolina University

"Peter de Silva is a leader with a big heart, a big soul, and a heap of humanity. Read *Taking Stock* to learn and be inspired to lead in these critical times. The book is approachable without hype or pretense. It is an account of a true leader in a Midwestern city. This book about community leadership is worth your time and attention."
—**Bernard Franklin**, 2022 Fellow, Advanced Leadership Initiative, Harvard University

"Peter de Silva reminds us it is never too late to be *Taking Stock* in our lives. He shares his personal mosaic and how he found the courage at Harvard to unveil his secret and dedicate his third chapter to the discovery of a cure."
—**Linda Rebrovick**, corporate board director, Harvard University Edmond & Lily Safra Center for Ethics Advisory Board & 2021 Fellow, Advanced Leadership Initiative, Harvard University

"In *Taking Stock*, Peter concisely and generously shares timeless lessons for principled leaders. It's a practical and actionable how-to guide for successful leaders, regardless of their career stage, industry, or organization size. Crisply written, *Taking Stock* should be required reading in business schools everywhere."

—**Gerry Lopez**, former president and CEO, AMC Theatres

"Peter has dedicated his life and efforts to four things: family, faith, business success, and giving back. His impact has been widespread, intentional, influential, and meaningful. *Taking Stock* provides personal and compelling insight into Peter's caring nature and unique leadership contributions. A must read."

—**Jeanette Prenger,** Founder and CEO, ECCO Select

"*Taking Stock* is our invitation to follow Peter de Silva on his journey to becoming a great leader and man. We see him making choices when he encounters the road sign DANGER AHEAD, regarding his health, and we see how those choices shaped him. Along the way, we see more and more people—family, associates, and customers—willing and happy to climb aboard and follow Peter's lead to the next stop. At every turn, there is a lesson to learn. Chief among them is that trusting relationships, built on mutual respect, inspire others to follow you. Great leaders understand this. Peter de Silva is a great leader."

—**Sylvester (Sly) James**, co-founder, Wickham James Strategies & Solutions; former mayor of Kansas City, Missouri

"Persistence through adversity, a willingness to work and think hard, and a belief in the power of ethical leadership describe Peter de Silva's professional career and personal character. His story in *Taking Stock* is a compelling read and is highly instructive. Peter de Silva is what the best of American business leaders, and outstanding American citizens, look like."

—**Peter J. Travers**, managing member, Chase Field LLC; chair, board of trustees, National Review Institute

"*Taking Stock* reveals the art of leadership while showing us real-world situations and events—good and challenging—that made Peter a leader in

the financial world and in life. He is someone we can all relate to and look up to as we pursue a life of meaning, impact, and purpose."
—**Randy Freer**, president and CEO, Teton Ridge; former CEO, Hulu, 2021 Fellow, Advanced Leadership Initiative, Harvard University

"My longtime friend, Peter de Silva, has put together a compelling account of how he overcame a serious physical problem and became a highly successful leader of one of our nation's top retail financial companies."
—**Christopher "Kit" Bond**, former US Senator, Missouri

"A young adult pushing a wheelbarrow laden with construction debris could be considered a metaphor for working hard to get ahead. It is an apt metaphor for Peter de Silva. This was literally how he started forty-three years ago in our professional relationship. That relationship became a lifelong friendship. And it was an apt metaphor for his career journey."
—**Roger Lockwood**, chair, Lockwood/McKinnon Company

"Despite overwhelming odds against success caused by Charcot-Marie-Tooth disease (CMT), Peter persevered to become an inspirational, accomplished, and successful business leader. *Taking Stock* is a fascinating look at his ferociously positive mindset for conquering adversity with time-tested principles and integrity."
—**Patrick Livney**, founder and chair, Charcot-Marie-Tooth Research Foundation (CMTRF)

"Peter has written a terrific book on the leadership skills he learned throughout his highly successful career. He shares these lessons in a highly personal way, putting everything into context and exposing himself as a leader and a human being."
—**Len Stecklow**, former Fidelity Investments and TD Ameritrade executive

"Peter quickly rises to the top in any consideration as a conservative, a Christian, an investment adviser, and an American."
—**Stephen Plaster**, chair and CEO, Evergreen Investments

"Infused with hard-won wisdom, Peter de Silva's *Taking Stock* is an invitation to reflect on and refine your professional and personal compass. He offers his own well-traveled map of key leadership principles as a guide. If you care deeply about your impact and reputation as a principled leader and seek long-term happiness as you grow your career, put this book on your required reading list."

—**Karen Fenaroli**, founder and CEO, Fenaroli & Associates; serial entrepreneur and boardroom C-suite coach

"In *Taking Stock*, Peter's reflections reveal the heart, soul, and character of a man continually invested in changing our world for the better. This work is a true treasure, filled with gems of wisdom and advice from Peter's vast business and life experiences. *Taking Stock* calls on us all to better reflect on our lives and our opportunities to enrich the lives of those around us."

—**The Reverend Tim Merrill**, founder, Watu Moja; 2021 Fellow, Advanced Leadership Initiative, Harvard University

"*Taking Stock* gave me new insights on how special Peter de Silva is—as a business leader and a Charcot-Marie-Tooth (CMT) patient. His largely silent struggles with CMT have clearly made Peter a more empathetic and inclusive leader. The book also offered me, as a mother of a young woman with CMT, a much greater appreciation for the often nuanced physical and emotional challenges of this often-invisible disease."

—**Cleary Simpson**, CEO, Charcot-Marie-Tooth Research Foundation

"A requisite read for any leader, *Taking Stock* is a master plan of de Silva's ten proven principles for successful ethical leadership."

—**Tom Chulick**, former chair and CEO, UMB Bank St. Louis and president of the Midwest Region

"Having had the pleasure of working with Peter in community and corporate settings, I know him as an effective, principled, and caring leader. He has made a difference in many lives. We can learn much from his journey and the insights he imparts."

—**Tom Butch**, former financial services executive and community leader

TAKING STOCK

*10 Life and Leadership Principles
from My Seat at the Table*

Peter J. de Silva

TAKING STOCK

10 Life and Leadership Principles from My Seat at the Table

© 2023 Peter J. de Silva

Limit of Liability/Disclaimer of Warranty: The publisher and the author make no representations or warranties with respect to the accuracy or completeness of the contents of this work and specifically disclaim all warranties, including without limitation warranties of fitness for a particular purpose. No warranty may be created or extended by sales or promotional materials. The advice, strategies and principles contained herein may not be suitable for every situation. This work is sold with the understanding that neither the author nor the publisher engaged in rendering legal, accounting, or other professional services. If professional assistance is required, the services of a competent professional person should be sought. Neither the publisher nor the author shall be liable for damages arising herefrom. The fact that an organization or website is referred to in this work as a citation and/or a potential source of further information does not mean that the author or the publisher endorses the information that the organization or website may provide or recommendations it may make.

To contact the author, Peter J. de Silva, visit

- Website: peterjdesilva.com
- Email: peter@peterjdesilva.com
- LinkedIn: http://linkedin.com/in/peter-j-desilva
- Business Facebook: facebook.com/peterjdesilvaauthor
- Personal Facebook: facebook.com/peter.desilva.104
- Twitter: @peterjdesilva
- Instagram: peterjdesilva

To contact the publisher, Gravitas Press, visit www.GravitasPress.com

Hardcover (Jacket) ISBN: 979-8-9878224-0-1
Hardcover (Case Laminate) ISBN: 979-8-9878224-3-2
Paperback ISBN: 979-8-9878224-1-8
eBook ISBN: 979-8-9878224-2-5

Book strategist: Bonnie Budzowski, Gravitas Press

Cover & Interior Design by: Melissa Farr, melissa@backporchcreative.com

Dedication

To Michelle, Christine, and Sarah for their belief in me and their constant support throughout our life journey together.

To aspiring leaders everywhere as they undertake their own leadership journeys and carve out their own path.

Table of Contents

Acknowledgments — *xiii*
Foreword — *xv*

Chapter 1 – A Powerful Leadership Metaphor: Mosaics — 1

Chapter 2 – My Lifelong Challenge: Charcot-Marie-Tooth Disease — 9

Chapter 3 – From Wheelbarrows to Wall Street: My Leadership Path — 23

    Personal and Professional Timeline — 31

Chapter 4 – Learning, Stretching, and Making My Way: Fidelity — 35

    Near Failure Is a Much Better Teacher Than Actual Failure — 50

    Model of a Visionary Leader: Ned Johnson — 56

Chapter 5 – Growing Up as a Consequential Leader: UMB Financial Corporation — 61

    Developing Emerging Talent with Fences — 73

    Three Zones of Control — 85

Chapter 6 – Discovering a New World of Leadership Possibilities: Kansas City — 91

    The Power of Enduring Relationships in All Aspects of Life — 95

    Notable Cause in Kansas City — 108

10 Life and Leadership Principles from My Seat at the Table — 113

Chapter 7 – The Evolving Crisis of Leadership: A Trifecta of Pressures — 121

    Five Cs of Credit — 125

Chapter 8 – Maintaining Perspective through Adversity:
Scottrade Financial Services 133

A Short History of the Discount Brokerage Industry 137

Chapter 9 – Driving Positive Change in a Sea of Ambiguity:
TD Ameritrade 155

Four Recommendations for Building Trust 163

Chapter 10 – Navigating Life's Third Chapter: Harvard University 185

Board Positions Come through Multiple Channels 190

Fundraising Alone Will Never Bring About Needed
Social Change 198

Chapter 11 – Anticipating New Patterns of Growth:
Wrapping Things Up 211

Afterword 217

About the Author *229*
A Special Bonus from Peter *233*

Acknowledgments

Although I wrote this book over a period of eighteen months, it involved taking stock of a sixty-year span of my life. Along the way, I repeatedly bumped into people who had profoundly and positively influenced my life. I want to acknowledge them here.

My parents, Norman and Margaret de Silva, provided an unconditionally loving and secure foundation, along with their examples of integrity, compassion, and community service. My parents gave me the courage I needed to persevere through many of life's most challenging obstacles.

At each key juncture in my adulthood, my wife, Michelle, has been beside me, listening, supporting me, and imparting wisdom. Michelle is a true partner, an amazing mother, a friend to all, and an exceptional human being.

My beautiful daughters, Christine and Sarah, have always been and continue to be the lights of my life. If I could make just one good investment, I would want it to be in them. The courage and zest with which my daughters pursue their interests inspires me.

My siblings—Norman, Lynne, and Bill—have given me unyielding love and support. Their loving jabs have kept me grounded and allowed me to spread my wings and become the whole person I am today.

These pages are filled with stories of mentors who took risks on me, believing in me and enriching my life and leadership. These include Fred Knapp, Rodger Riney, Roger Lockwood, Terry Dunn, Cliff Illig, Greg Graves, Roshann Parris, Karen Fenaroli, Mayor Sylvester "Sly" James, Clyde Wendel, and Tim Hockey. I also want to acknowledge Richard "Dick" Jones, Donald Hall, Jr., Senator Kit Bond, Stephen Plaster, Jeanette Prenger, Gene Diederich, Peggy Dunn, Anne St. Peter, and Adele Hall. Many others have knowingly or unknowingly enriched the mosaic of my life by word or example. I am profoundly aware that any measure of success I have achieved is a credit to each of these people.

My niece, Amy, was the first person in my life to demonstrate the courage to go public with her CMT disease in an effort to help others. Pat Livney, Susan Ruediger, and Cleary Simpson kept encouraging me to become a leader in the pursuit of treatments and cures for CMT. They never gave up on me. My experience at the Harvard Advanced Leadership Initiative and, fittingly, Michelle's words of challenge to me were the final impetus to take the plunge.

Becoming a public face for CMT and co-chairing a $10 million fundraising campaign has been a life-altering experience for me. Those who live life to the fullest, despite their struggles with CMT, inspire me every day.

Bonnie Budzowski, my thought partner and publisher with Gravitas Press, was my companion during the eighteen-month journey in *Taking Stock*. Without her, this book would just be an idea constantly rattling around in my head. Together, Bonnie and I wrestled with ideas, clarified concepts, and wove seemingly disparate thoughts into a cohesive whole. Bonnie's patience, focus, and understanding, along with her kindness and compassion, were instrumental in making this book a reality.

Foreword

From an early age to the present, Peter de Silva has suffered the effects of a chronic disease; yet, through grit, intelligence, and a sense of humor, he overcame its drag on his life. He became a successful leader in finance and banking, embracing ever greater responsibility and difficult challenges. In doing so, Peter became a force for change and improvement at the companies he joined and the communities that adopted him.

I met Peter when he joined UMB Financial Corporation in Kansas City, Missouri, as its president and COO. I was president of the Federal Reserve Bank of Kansas City at the time. I watched as Peter shared business and community leadership with the Kemper family and worked to maintain the strong financial standing and independence of an iconic regional bank.

At UMB, Peter helped build a culture of service while maintaining the bank's local roots and financial standing in a time of industry consolidation and Wall Street's insistence on financial return above safety. UMB bank was one of the few regional banks that neither required nor took government financial assistance. This pursuit of independent thinking and commitment to excellence is demonstrated throughout Peter's book.

I also witnessed Peter's commitment to the Kansas City region. He notes his role with the chamber of commerce, but more than that, he established ties to various Kansas City communities and joined others in promoting the region as a center for commerce and a hub for transporting goods throughout the country. Not surprisingly, Peter supported education by taking on a leadership role, supporting the area's local colleges.

Finally, Peter recognized when it was time to leave the bank and take on new challenges. He did so with grace and his ever-present positive attitude that reflect so much of the character of a leader.

From his experiences and life challenges, Peter has developed a set of principles that guide his actions and have served well to make him a reliable, effective, and ethical leader. I won't list each principle here since his book does a far better job than I can, but I will highlight those that most impressed me.

Peter determined early in his career that success requires that you recruit and inspire talented people committed to a common set of goals. He looked for individuals capable of learning, doing the job in the right spirit, and doing it well. He understood that leaders can accomplish great things with the help of others. Peter recognized early the necessity of building and communicating a meaningful vision and then providing the resources to achieve the vision. He also recognized that he had to serve as an example, inspiring and enabling followers to do great things. Sadly, many leaders fail to recognize this simple but critical principle.

Another of his principles is the all-important one of recognizing success, generously sharing credit, and rewarding good work. So many individuals in leadership roles see their staff's hard work and success as loyalty owed them. As Peter makes clear with examples throughout the book, a leader's first and last duty is loyalty to the team. Only when trust is built among team members is the team able to serve the public and their investors best.

A final principle, or theme, running through this book can be best summarized by the saying: If something is inevitable, embrace it. Peter has experienced great change throughout his long career. He instinctively knows how to accept change, how to cope with the uncertainty surrounding it, and how to help others confront uncertainty with confidence.

Change sometimes involves unpleasant surprises. It is the leader's responsibility to manage through the uncertainty, sorting through possible opportunities as well as its threats. Most difficult are those times when a leader must determine when change is beyond his or her power to harness, then communicate its effects to those whose lives will be disrupted. This is never an easy task, but it is still a leader's duty to perform.

In these pages, you'll see that Peter does something that leaders too seldom do in today's competitive, me-first business world. He references a higher power. Given his personal journey facing setbacks and successes, Peter recognized the importance of caring for others, and he quotes Scripture and what can be learned from it. In doing so, he relies on lessons that reflect millennia of experience, which—to borrow a modern concept—represent long-known best practices in leadership.

Taking Stock is more than a primer on leadership and more than a memoir. It is a series of lessons on leadership gained through hands-on experience as Peter confronted personal obstacles to achieve success for himself and those he led.

I think you will enjoy Peter's story as you learn about leadership—what it is, how it develops, and what it can accomplish when based on sound principles.

Tom Hoenig
Distinguished Senior Fellow, Mercatus Center;
former chair, FDIC and former president of Federal Reserve Bank of Kansas City
January 24, 2023, Arlington, Virginia

Chapter 1

A Powerful Leadership Metaphor: Mosaics

The beauty and intricacy of mosaics, tiles, and stained-glass windows fascinate me. I've been fortunate enough to visit some exceptional examples: Notre Dame in Paris; St. Patrick's Cathedral in New York City; the Cathedral Basilica of St. Louis, Missouri; and the Blue Mosque and the Hagia Sophia Grand Mosque, both in Istanbul. St. George, my childhood parish in Dartmouth, Massachusetts, had a beautiful stained-glass window above the altar with a lamb at the center, representing the Lamb of God. I stared at that window repeatedly during Masses, seeking its meaning.

In a mosaic, thousands, if not millions, of individual pieces all work together in perfect harmony to tell a single story, to create a vibrant picture. While each piece individually may not seem significant in and of itself, each is a critical part of the whole. Sometimes you need to look carefully to find and interpret the story imbedded in a mosaic, but the story is always there.

I think of each life as a personal mosaic. My own mosaic is made up of all the experiences and people I've encountered on my life journey so far. Our mosaics comprise the people who touched us, and, more profoundly, *how* those people affected our views, perspectives, and development. A person may leave an impression, a set of values, a belief system, or a set of actions that we might want—or not want—to emulate.

The pieces of a mosaic are often shards from smashed, shattered, weathered, and forgotten objects. These are used to create something beautifully textured, unique, and personal. In other words, the shambles and missteps of life make the mosaic more beautiful and meaningful.

While the patterns in our personal mosaics become more defined as we mature, the picture—the art of our lives—cannot be entirely complete until we draw our last breath. The last words of encouragement—that you offer to someone or that someone offers to you—may find their way onto both mosaics. A mosaic missing even a single element of your life is akin to a jigsaw puzzle missing a key piece. Think of your completed mosaic as a gift to your family and friends to cherish once you are gone. It is a thing of beauty.

In writing this book, I'm sharing my personal mosaic. It may seem like a collection of unrelated experiences—pieces of glass, some bright and vibrant, some dark and brooding. Most of those detailed here are about my life's work thus far, inside and outside the parameters of my job descriptions. I expect to have many productive years ahead of me, and my mosaic will continue to be shaped by experiences, lessons, and observations.

This book's title, *Taking Stock*, has multiple levels of meaning. I'm old enough and seasoned enough as a leader to see how certain experiences, individuals, and decisions I've made have resulted in patterns that stand in relief in my mosaic—and to believe that I have some valuable insights to share.

Taking Stock is also an invitation to take time to reflect on where you are, what got you to this point, and where you might be headed. Taking the time to take stock of your career, your relationships, and your life's purpose is always a worthwhile endeavor. I encourage you to reflect on your ever-evolving mosaic as I share my story and the lessons it imparts.

The most obvious of these lessons is the brief compendium of leadership principles showcased in the center of the book and highlighted in multiple ways throughout. In *Taking Stock*, I'm defining my principles of leadership success much as Stephen Covey famously did in his work *Principle-Centered*

Leadership. I have great admiration for Covey. Don't think for a minute that I'm trying to put myself above him, or even beside him. Covey is the master. But Covey and I are different. I don't come at the topic of leadership from an academic or purely intellectual standpoint. I have been a leadership practitioner for over thirty-five years, with all that goes along with that. My experiences are from the real world in real time. I have made many mistakes and learned from them. I have observed many others, choosing which characteristics to emulate and which to cast aside.

When Covey talks about principled leaders, he speaks of characteristics. My principles in *Taking Stock* are more along the lines of behaviors or habits. They are structured similarly to Covey's list in *The 7 Habits of Highly Effective People*. Rather than compete with Covey's work, I look at the topic from a different—and I trust complementary—angle: my own experiences. I'm simply sifting through my personal life and leadership journey to date.

Given Covey's books and those of other distinguished leadership authors out there, you might wonder what makes mine worthwhile and special. While the heart of this book is the leadership principles, the context is my personal mosaic, the story of how my shards of glass worked together to shape the leader and person I am today.

Two factors are unique to my professional story. One is that from an early age, I have been challenged by Charcot-Marie-Tooth disease (CMT), a progressive, degenerative disease involving the peripheral nervous system. Symptoms include pain, muscle wasting, decreased muscle size, decreased sensation, hammertoes, and high arches, to name a few. The disease is hereditary and, to date, incurable.

CMT not only affected my choice of a career, but it also led to choices in how I presented myself throughout that career and in my personal relationships. Taking stock now, at a mature point in my life, I'd advise my younger self to look at those choices differently.

Also unique to me is that my career has included a seat at the table with some of the financial industry's most iconic leaders during many industry crises, including the stock market crash of 1987, the 1999 dot-com bubble and bust, the 2008 financial crisis, a global pandemic, and the rise and fall of the discount brokerage industry. I worked alongside and was mentored by some of the smartest, shrewdest, and most ethical leaders imaginable during these stressful times. For that I am grateful as well as forever changed.

For example, I worked with Crosby Kemper Jr. and his executive team at UMB Financial Corporation (formerly United Missouri Bancshares) prior to and during the 2008 financial crisis. Thanks to Crosby's strongly held beliefs about the wisdom of maintaining prudent lending practices, UMB made the decision not to make risky subprime mortgages and shaky commercial loans. While these loans were legal and very profitable, they were not right.

Crosby never accepted the premise that it was okay to put more debt on individuals or businesses than they could service. Doing so might improve earnings in the short term, but it was certain to end in disaster when the tide turned. As a well-capitalized bank with a moderate risk profile, we didn't do this. Neither did we succumb to pressure, at the height of the financial crisis, to take bailout money we didn't want or need from the US government. Leading by time-tested principles, we were the better for it.

Watching how the executives at other firms made choices, leading up to and following the crisis, upset me. My discomfort caused me to reflect upon leadership ethics and the forces that derail them. I put great personal effort into trying to understand how so many leaders had gone so wrong at the expense of so many innocent people and businesses.

In 2010, I was asked to prepare and present a paper on ethics at a leadership symposium at the United States Army's Command and General Staff College at Fort Leavenworth, Kansas. This is the graduate school for the United States Army and sister service officers, interagency representatives, and international military officers. Notable graduates include Generals George C. Marshall, Omar Bradley, George Patton, and David Petraeus.

The title of my paper and speech was "Examining Ethics in the Face of Great Challenge: Lessons in Principled Leadership from the Financial Crisis." During that period, I found myself in high demand as a speaker at colleges and universities across the Midwest. Americans desperately wanted to understand where we had gone so terribly wrong.

As my career progressed, I had my share of ethical leadership challenges in executive positions at Scottrade and TD Ameritrade as the financial industry was in great flux. Fortunately, the senior teams in both organizations were principled leaders.

I did, however, once find myself in an ethical bind that had no easy solution, one that kept me extremely uncomfortable for months. When TD Ameritrade purchased Scottrade, I had been president of the latter for less than ten months. Almost immediately following the deal announcement, I was an active member of the team planning the client integration effort.

Meanwhile, Tim Hockey, TD Ameritrade's CEO, asked me to join his leadership team upon the deal closing. My start date was contingent on the deal closing date, which we could not know with any precision at that time. Neither of us thought this would be a big problem as we both anticipated quick regulatory approval. As events unfolded, the needed approvals process stretched for months longer than expected, making for a tenuous situation.

I kept the commitment I made to keep my upcoming position a secret. While hiding this fact from the incumbent, I was also hiding it from the world at large—while working alongside the incumbent on a regular basis. I was so uncomfortable with the situation that I looked up the word deceit in the dictionary to see if it applied to me in this case. In the literal sense, it did. Yet I was obligated to keep my commitment to my new boss. Any other choice would break trust and create chaos and anxiety for associates and other stakeholders.

Less than two years into my role at TD Ameritrade, the decision was made to sell the company to Charles Schwab. Once the deal was closed in the fall of 2020, after significant work planning the integration, I was severed by Charles Schwab with the complicating factor of a two-year noncompete agreement. That essentially put me out of the industry in which I had spent nearly thirty years.

Suddenly, I was an executive without a base and without the influential platform and resources I was long accustomed to. When the volume of emails and calls for help abruptly ended, I felt deflated and out of equilibrium. And I had to decide what to do next.

Would I pursue another large corporate leadership position or consider it time to do something entirely different? I knew that my leadership skills were transferrable to other industries, but would someone take a chance on me? I was, after all, now in what sociologist Sara Lawrence-Lightfoot named "the third chapter" in her book *The Third Chapter: Passion, Risk, and Adventure in the 25 Years After 50*.

From Lawrence-Lightfoot's perspective, everything you have done—the skills you have acquired, combined with the experiences you have had until the age of forty-nine—prepares you for the years spanning fifty to seventy-five. These are the years during which you will make your most important societal contributions. There is, of course, a fourth chapter of life, but that is not quite as pleasant to contemplate.

At the time I was severed from Schwab, I was already—at least in terms of my age—into my third chapter. Like most people in this age group, I was still energetic. I wanted to continue to make meaningful contributions to the world. I was, however, at a decision point regarding where and how best to make those contributions.

After much consideration, I applied to and was appointed as a Harvard University Fellow in the highly regarded Advanced Leadership Initiative (ALI). This is a year-long, interdisciplinary program designed to "unleash the potential of experienced leaders to help solve society's most pressing challenges." To me, this program represented an opportunity to add even deeper meaning to my life and work. It was also an opportunity to add other dimensions to my leadership mosaic.

One feature of the ALI program is that the Fellow's spouse or life partner is invited to participate in all elements of the program. My wife, Michelle, could fully participate as much as she wanted with me in the program, and she could pursue her own interests. She would have all the resources across Harvard at her disposal. We were both thrilled with this opportunity to do something together while also building on our individual strengths.

Michelle and I completed the ALI program in 2022, and I look forward to sharing with you later in the book the social impact challenges that each of us has decided to undertake.

One of the many benefits of the ALI program is the opportunity to step back, take stock, and reset for what comes next. I was privileged to do this while interacting with brilliant professors and diverse, accomplished leaders from around the world. My perspectives were stretched and enriched every day. I discovered I had a lot to contribute as well as a lot to take in.

I've had a long-standing desire to articulate my principles of leadership success. At various times, I jotted down thoughts, refining and combining principles for clarity. I finished the work in 2021 and 2022 as I was participating in ALI and writing this book. Those principles are at the heart of what I want to share in these pages.

I wrote this book for current and aspiring leaders who want to hear real-world, practical lessons from someone who has been on the leadership front lines for more than thirty-five years. From one perspective, I'm telling my story as a seasoned executive who had a seat at the table during a tumultuous time, and who has taken the time to reflect deeply on what he's seen, and drawn clear conclusions. From another perspective, I've just spent time at Harvard, surrounded by gifted and accomplished academic, business, political, and social impact leaders. I've learned that the more I learn, the more I realize how little I know. I'm okay with that. After all, my mosaic is not yet complete.

For now, I invite you to take stock with me. If you invest the time and energy to consider the ideas in this book, you'll walk away with important lessons about the true nature of leadership, including a set of leadership principles you and others can easily understand and put to work.

Chapter 2

My Lifelong Challenge: Charcot-Marie-Tooth Disease

It was the equivalent of the ninth inning in my Dartmouth Youth Athletic Association Little League game. Our team, the Athletics, was down one run with two outs, with runners on second and third. It was my turn at bat. My coach and teammates were exhorting me: "Just make contact with the ball, just let the ball hit the bat." That's all I had to do. Easy for them to say.

Standing at the plate, all of age twelve, I was as nervous as I could be. The first pitch was wide. I held my swing. Maybe I could walk my way onto base. I saw the next pitch coming right down the middle of the plate, but I was too afraid to swing. It was strike one. On the third pitch, I closed my eyes, put the bat out and, by some stroke of good luck, the ball collided with the bat. With reasonably good speed, the ball was heading to the area between the second baseman and the shortstop. For a moment, it even looked like the ball might make it through to the outfield.

Terrified, I took off for first base. The runners on second and third both headed for home. The second baseman picked up the ball cleanly and was about to throw it over to the first baseman. The fans were cheering. I thought we might win or at least tie the game on my hit. Then, the inevitable happened: I tripped and fell to the ground in a cloud of dust. I was easily thrown out at first base. The game was over. We lost. I cried about that play all night long. It's still a nightmare memory for me.

As a young person, I tripped and fell on a regular basis. My parents and I knew something was not right, but I had not yet been diagnosed with Charcot-Marie-Tooth (CMT) disease, an inherited genetic abnormality. CMT results in abnormalities in the nerves that supply the feet, hands, legs, and arms, affecting both the motor and sensory nerves. Although CMT typically first appears in adolescence or early adulthood, it can occur as a spontaneous mutation at any time in the life of an otherwise healthy individual. It is a lifelong debilitating disease that accelerates over time. No treatments or cures are currently available.

CMT was first identified and described by neurologists Jean-Martin Charcot, Pierre Marie, and Howard Henry Tooth in 1886. It is the most prevalent disease within a category classified in the US as rare diseases, affecting approximately one in 2,500 people worldwide. CMT is present in all races, ethnicities, genders, and countries.

While individuals generally do not die as a direct result of CMT, it is a contributor to early death in some cases. If someone falls down a staircase, hits his or her head and dies, the death certificate will likely say the person died from head trauma, not CMT. While CMT did not technically kill the person, the lack of stability and balance because of CMT was likely to be the reason the person fell in the first place.

Approximately 150,000 cases of CMT exist in the US, and over three million cases can be found worldwide. It is widely believed that these case numbers are significantly understated as most physicians are not familiar with CMT, leaving many affected individuals undiagnosed or misdiagnosed. This is especially true in less developed countries where the health care systems are not as advanced as those in the US, Western Europe, and some parts of Asia.

Individuals with CMT struggle with constant pain, weakness, and a lack of strength throughout their extremities, among other debilitating symptoms. The disease manifests differently from person to person, with effects ranging from moderate to life-altering. As a progressive disease, the manifestations grow as the individual ages. Many people who suffer from

CMT need leg braces, orthotics, and other forms of mobility assistance, sometimes even wheelchairs. These are currently the only noninvasive options for CMT. In some cases, surgery is also an option to help improve mobility and stability.

I am the third of four children born to Norman and Margaret de Silva and a member of an extended family affected by CMT. I have an older brother, an older sister, and a younger brother. My father was a successful manager of retail department stores and at one point owned his own business. My mother was a registered nurse in the maternity ward at St. Luke's Hospital in New Bedford, Massachusetts. My family was neither poor nor rich. We were a middle-class American family simply trying to make our way in the world. While we never had all that we wanted, we had everything we needed: family, friends, and faith. We never took vacations, so we never missed them. We were taught that hard work, ethics, thrift, grit, and personal sacrifice were important personal characteristics. We were a loving family, with a safe environment in which to grow and become ourselves. I will always be grateful for the love and values that set the foundation for my life.

Our family heritage is distinctive in that all four of my grandparents were of Azorean descent. Both maternal grandmothers and my maternal grandfather were born on the islands. My paternal grandfather's family was also from the Azores, although they had left the Azores and arrived in the US earlier. He was born in Cottage City, Massachusetts. Since 1907, this community on Martha's Vineyard has been known as Oak Bluffs.

The Azores, officially the Autonomous Region of the Azores, is one of two autonomous regions of Portugal (along with Madeira). It is an archipelago comprised of nine volcanic islands in the North Atlantic Ocean with a current total population of approximately 250,000. It has been a proud but poor area where agriculture, fishing, and more recently tourism are the dominant industries. The islands are blessed with natural beauty and carry the nickname "the Hawaii of the Atlantic."

My ancestors left the island of São Miguel in the early 1900s and came to the US for better opportunities and a better life. They arrived in Boston and made their way to New Bedford, where many other Portuguese and Azorean immigrants had gone to make their living in either the textile mills or in the fishing industry. Even today, more than 50 percent of New Bedford's residents claim Portuguese ancestry. The Portuguese language is spoken freely, and many long-standing Azorean and Portuguese traditions are still followed.

Growing up, I did not have much perspective as to what it meant to be Azorean/Portuguese. My parents and grandparents spoke fluent English (although they would sometimes revert to Portuguese when they did not want the children to know what they were saying), and we were proud Americans of Portuguese descent.

I grew up in Dartmouth, Massachusetts, just a few miles west of New Bedford. Dartmouth is a beautiful seaside community with a proud maritime past. However, it was not a very diverse place to grow up. There were many times in school when other children would pick on me solely because my family was from "the islands" (even though it was a generation ago), as somehow that fact made our family—and me—inferior. There were certain derogatory words that were used to describe us. I did not understand at the time that kids learned bigotry at a very young age. There were very few people of color in the community. My first encounter with an African American student did not occur until high school. Such was life in the late sixties and early seventies.

My sister, Lynne, was the first in our family to be officially diagnosed with CMT. She was around thirteen or fourteen years old at the time, and her diagnosis came as a surprise. She endured numerous surgeries in her teenage years to ease her symptoms.

Since CMT is a hereditary disease with a fifty-fifty chance of offspring receiving it from the affected parent, there was the risk that my brothers and I had the disease as well. While my brothers and I were never formally tested, it was quite obvious at that point due to physical deformities that

I had CMT. My brothers did not exhibit any symptoms at that time. My diagnosis led to a lifetime of physical and emotional challenges with this disease. CMT is unrelenting.

We suspect the disease came through my father's family. Since my grandfather on that side died in his early thirties, however, we don't have enough information to know how far the disease goes back in that part of our family line. It turned out that my father had CMT too, but it only began to present symptoms later in his life. My dad was an amazing athlete in his younger days. He showed no physical signs of CMT until later in life. That's the thing about CMT: It can lie dormant until one day it begins to present itself.

During my freshman year of high school, my parents decided it was time for me to face significant reconstructive surgery on both legs, both ankles, and both feet. I was operated on multiple times by Arthur Pappas, the famous Red Sox baseball team medical director (1978–2002), at Boston Children's Hospital.

My parents decided I should have both legs operated on, nearly back to back, which, in retrospect, was probably a bad idea. The surgeries were extremely long, complicated, and painful. I endured a long road to recovery, with seemingly endless physical therapy. At one point, I was in a wheelchair for almost six months. For most of my freshman year in high school, I was tutored at home.

Despite the challenges and time lost from the surgeries, I am glad my parents made the choice for me to have the procedures. The surgeries have given me much better mobility and stability than I might otherwise have had.

In the fall of 1984, life dealt me another medical blow. By this time, I had nearly completed my business degree at Southeastern Massachusetts University (SMU). I was living at home with my parents and younger brother, working at my first true job at Cinema 140, in addition to attending SMU.

One day, feeling cold, sweaty, and generally unwell, I went to my primary care doctor, expecting him to prescribe medication for the flu or other virus. Instead, after a cursory physical exam, Dr. Ross instructed me to check myself into the local hospital right away.

Multiple tests over the next few days revealed a mass the size of a football on my left side. Doctors were not sure, but my condition was potentially leukemia or another type of cancer. My parents and I chose to have me transferred to Boston Children's Hospital where more qualified specialists could be consulted. I was the oldest person in the ward. Because I had been treated at Children's Hospital for my CMT as a child, I could be treated there for the rest of my life.

Following more tests, the doctors determined I had a giant hydronephrosis, a swelling due to partial blockage of the left kidney, that may have been present in some form since birth. I did not have cancer; nonetheless, my condition was very serious.

Arnold Colodny, a surgeon specializing in pediatric urology, visited me the evening before the necessary surgery. Unsure of what he would find the next day, he requested permission to make a game-time decision about trying to repair my left kidney or removing it altogether. I agreed.

Before I was wheeled to the operating room early the next morning, a priest came to visit me, which was both comforting and scary. We prayed together for a safe and speedy recovery.

When Dr. Colodny made the incision on my left side, I'm told a mass the size of a football fell onto the table. This was the result of an almost total blockage of my left kidney's drainage function. He worked for many hours, much longer than expected, to remove the mass and attempt to repair the kidney function to some degree.

Although there was extensive damage, the doctor felt it was worth the effort to save the kidney, even if I only ended up with 50 percent function on that side. I spent multiple weeks in the hospital recovering. Over the next few months, I contracted pneumonia, bled extensively, and suffered several other serious medical issues.

Roughly six months post-surgery, it became evident that the surgical procedure to restore limited function to the left kidney had been unsuccessful.

A second reconstructive surgery, followed by another painful recovery, was also unsuccessful.

A final surgical procedure, a nephrectomy, removed what remained of my left kidney. The completion of that surgery was in many ways a fresh beginning for me. Once the recovery was complete, I felt better than I had in a long time. I was ready to conquer the world.

During this time, I learned an enduring leadership principle, one that would be a strong presence in my mosaic and remain with me for my entire career. While I was undergoing treatment for my kidney problems, I was working as a manager for Lockwood/Friedman Film Corporation's Cinema 140 under the leadership of co-owner Roger Lockwood and general manager, Gordon McKinnon.

Not once did either of these leaders ask how much my illness was going to cost the company in terms of lost productivity. Nor did they ask how much it was going to cost the then-small company in terms of increased health insurance premiums down the road. They only expressed concern about my health and well-being, first as a person and second as an employee. They understood long before I did that if you take care of your employees, your employees will take care of the customers, and the rest will take care of itself. More to come on this principle later in the book.

I never considered allowing my CMT and medical setbacks to define me as a person or leader. In large part, this is because my parents taught me not to, by word and example. My father's challenges with CMT came later in life for him, but those challenges were severe. Due to a confluence of different medical conditions, my father, in his fifties, was forced to have his left leg amputated below the knee. Before and after that, he taught me to push through adversity and do all I could with what life gave me to work with. Although he constantly struggled with walking and everyday tasks, Dad never complained.

My mother had an outsized influence on my life. She, too, believed that I should keep my medical challenges to myself and simply grit it out. After all, my health was no one else's business. At the same time, my mom had an ever-present compassionate side. She was endlessly supportive and protective of me, especially when others made fun of me, which occurred regularly.

When it became apparent that sports were not going to be a good outlet for me, Mom encouraged more appropriate activities. For example, she suggested I try music, beginning with piano. Unfortunately, I had a hard time with the raps on the knuckles I received from the nuns each time I made a mistake. I switched to the trumpet and joined the middle school band. I continued to play in high school—in the symphonic band and the marching band. I became one of the better trumpet players and was occasionally asked to do solos. Everything worked out well until marching band season, when marching in parades and around football fields was a big challenge. The pain was nearly unbearable, but as I had been taught, I pushed through it. I wasn't going to ask for any kind of accommodation.

Later in life, Michelle urged me to take up cycling as an athletic pursuit. I always cycled as a kid and agreed that it would be a good outlet for me. She challenged me to get in shape for my fortieth birthday by riding in the Pan-Mass Challenge® (PMC). The PMC is a two-day cycling event covering nearly 200 miles. PMC is the largest sports fundraiser in the world (in terms of dollars raised), bringing in more than $50 million annually. All proceeds benefit the Dana-Farber Cancer Institute in Boston.

I accepted Michelle's challenge. The first year I chose to undertake the one-day 100-mile route. I was not the fastest rider, but I finished, which was a big accomplishment for me. I went on to participate in many 200-mile fundraising rides, becoming a "Heavy Hitter" fundraiser for the organization.

I push forward in the ways I can because of how I was raised; plus, I have seen people in worse shape than I. If you want to see people with real challenges, go to Boston Children's Hospital and walk around the wards. The things you see will bring you to tears. For example, I remember being in a room with a boy named Tippy. Tippy had been shot in the head and was not expected to survive. Even today, I remember that young boy with a heavy heart. How blessed was I not to have something much worse.

I don't share stories of my medical challenges and family life looking for praise or pity but because these elements are core influences in my mosaic, important components of who I became and who I am today. CMT is an inescapable factor in my story.

To survive the many complicated surgeries and long periods of recovery, I developed fortitude and determination. Recovering from surgery and undergoing physical therapy, I spent a good chunk of my freshman year of high school being tutored at home. I learned to look for strength within myself rather than from others. I developed a tendency to work alone. It's not that I didn't like people or respect the talents of others, it's just that I developed the expectation that I would need to conquer any obstacles on my own. In retrospect, I see that this approach sometimes contrasted with my strong commitment to collaboration. I eventually came to realize the power of individuals working together as teams and the power of complementary strengths.

Even in high school, I was aware that CMT had not and would not affect my cognitive ability. If I made my living with my intellect and worked hard, I had as much of a chance of success as anyone. I didn't want others to see me as different. Nor did I want anyone to offer me a shortcut to success. You might say the de Silva family has a strong and stubborn streak of pride. That has its good side and its bad side.

My parents' influence played the largest part in my continuing choice to keep my medical challenges private, but it wasn't the only influence. As a kid, I was embarrassed about being "less than" in any way. Experiences such as the one on the Little League field and regularly being the last one picked for middle school dodgeball left me feeling insecure. I battled against that insecurity even during most of my adult years. I developed a drive to overcompensate and overachieve.

When I was leaving Lockwood/Friedman Film Corporation where I had been valued as a leader, I was worried that I might miss out on jobs or promotions because someone would assume that my condition meant I was unable to keep up with the demands of a leadership position.

There's no easy way to be partially open about CMT, so I kept mum about my condition with colleagues and friends, even close friends, for well over thirty years. I use orthotics to help me walk and I try not to remove my shoes in public. When anyone noticed that I was having more difficulty getting around than usual, I brushed it off by offering up a vague excuse about an old injury.

Over the years, I frequently struggled with the ethics of my secretiveness. I've always strived to be genuine, approachable, and authentic, and my secrecy often felt like a lie of omission. This left me with a sense of unease.

Ultimately, I concluded that the choice to keep silent about or disclose my medical condition was an issue of personal privacy rather than deception. I was convinced that CMT was a condition that concerned only the trio of Lynne, my father, and me—and we were dealing with it. Why did anyone else need to know about it?

Ultimately, it turned out that my perspective on the limited scope of CMT in my family was dead wrong. Lynne, my father, and I were only the earliest members in our family to show symptoms of the disease that is now ravishing my extended family. Without intervention, it threatens to strike my grandchildren and their children as well. I chill to think of it.

For decades, because of my need for secrecy about my CMT, I raised tens of millions of dollars for various charities while refusing to acknowledge and help my own community. Only in the third chapter of my life have I come to grips with the fact that my obstinate silence on the subject was a denial of a community to which I inherently belong. As a young person, I was more concerned about what I could lose by associating myself with that community than I was about what I could give.

My first job outside Lockwood/Friedman Film Corporation was at Fidelity Investments. While there, I met and began to date Michelle Garron. I came to love Michelle and wanted her to become my life partner. My secretiveness around CMT almost derailed the relationship. I was reluctant to tell Michelle about CMT, fearing the knowledge would somehow diminish me in her eyes. However, I realized that if this was the woman I was to marry, I needed to start off with complete honesty and transparency.

I remember the day I got up the courage to tell her about my condition. We had gone back to her apartment after having dinner, and I decided it was time. I was terrified that she might reject me. In fact, the opposite occurred.

Michelle embraced me and told me that CMT would not define me in her eyes. I would define myself. CMT was part of who I was, not what I was. In retrospect, I felt terrible about having doubted her support, but that is where I was at the time.

I was incredibly relieved over Michelle's reaction to my news. Where I was expecting rejection, Michelle met me with acceptance and support. She neither pulled back nor responded with pity. I asked her to keep my condition a secret, even from her family, and she agreed to do so. Over time, I let Michelle's family know about my condition. They, like Michelle, have been endlessly supportive.

Taking stock now, I wonder why I didn't reevaluate my expectations about how others might react to news of my CMT in light of Michelle's supportive response—but I didn't. I had a blind spot about this for many years. That blind spot likely resulted in some missed opportunities to forge some deeper relationships along the way.

Michelle and I married in December of 1989 and were later blessed with two beautiful daughters. Christine is currently twenty-nine; Sarah is twenty-six. These young women have always been the apples of my eye.

Christine was born in Boston in 1993. She moved with us to Cincinnati and then back to North Andover, Massachusetts, a few years later. Christine was about to enter sixth grade when we moved to Kansas City.

Once we moved to Kansas City, Michelle, Christine, and Sarah (born in 1996) spent the summers on Cape Cod at our house in Chatham. This is where Christine felt most at home and where she picked up her love of science and the oceans. She loved to walk the beaches—picking up shells, unusual rocks, and just about any kind of sea creature to investigate. Many of these sea creatures made it home to a small salt-water aquarium we kept for her collection.

Many evenings, Christine, Sarah, Michelle, and I went fishing together at the bridge on Bridge Street, catching sea robins, scup, and sometimes even a small striped bass or two, which are called schoolies. The oceans and a wide variety of watersports became a big part of Christine's life. When spring came in Kansas City, Christine was looking forward to being in Chatham for the summer.

It was no surprise that Christine chose to enroll at the University of Miami in its marine science program. Her path had seemed evident from an early age. It was and still is a joy for Michelle and me to share in her fascination, excitement, curiosity, and creativity.

I remember moving Christine into her dorm room on the campus of UMiami on one of the hottest days I've ever experienced. Michelle and I cried as we drove away, leaving our firstborn to her new adventures. Christine thrived at UMiami, joining the sailing team and becoming active in the marine science program. This is where she further developed her love of science, marine conservation, the oceans, and, eventually, sharks.

Today, Christine is an accomplished marine scientist. She works with a research-focused marine organization called Beneath the Waves and has been on Discovery Channel's *Shark Week* program several times. Recently, she and her business partner started Juice Robotics, with the goal of democratizing deep sea exploration. Christine is currently completing her master's in oceanography and her MBA at the University of Rhode Island. Michelle and I are extremely proud of her.

Sarah was born in 1996 in Cincinnati, Ohio. While we lived in Villa Hills, Kentucky, Good Samaritan Hospital was in downtown Cincinnati, so Sarah was born a Buckeye. Sarah was too young to remember any part of her Cincinnati experience, but pictures show that she was there.

Sarah's first vivid memories are of friends and family from North Andover, Massachusetts. She loved North Andover, where she went to school, played soccer, and built some wonderful friendships, including one with her lifelong friend Caroline Schmidt.

Sarah was about to enter the third grade when we moved from North Andover to Kansas City. She was sad to leave her friends and family behind. I remember reading some goodbye notes she exchanged with Caroline. They were heart-wrenching.

A kind, empathetic, and mischievous child, Sarah had many interests while growing up. These included sports, the ocean, sailing, and her family. Unlike Christine, it was unclear early on what Sarah's ultimate career pursuits might be. Eventually she gravitated toward the business world. I don't know if Sarah's interest in business came from observing what I do or from another source.

Sarah chose to attend Northeastern University, in Boston, as a business major with an emphasis on entrepreneurship. We dropped her off on a beautiful fall day. The air was clear and the winds were brisk. There was none of the unbearable heat that marked Christine's move into UMiami. But, just like when we dropped off Christine, Michelle and I cried on the way home.

It felt odd that Sarah moved back to Boston from Kansas City before Michelle and I did. We would visit our daughter in our home state while we were still living far away in Kansas City. There was something perverse in all this, but I guess that's the way it was meant to be. We would always have summers together on Cape Cod to look forward to.

Although Christine has shown no evidence of CMT to date, Sarah, unfortunately, exhibited signs at an early age. She was a late walker, which is typical of individuals with CMT, as is walking on tiptoes. Sarah tripped and fell often, just as I had. We laugh now about making Sarah wear a bicycle helmet when she was playing on our concrete driveway.

By the time she was three or four, it was clear that Sarah had the disease. Other than taking the steps to get Sarah the help she needed, I found it difficult to let the reality of her CMT sink in. Sarah's cousin, Amy, who is about Sarah's age, was also diagnosed with CMT around the same time.

Amy's symptoms caused extreme problems with her hands, limiting her activity and requiring surgeries. In light of her physical limitations, Amy poured her energy into developing her talent as a singer and being featured as a soloist at a young age.

I was in denial regarding Sarah and Amy's diagnoses. I was not yet ready to face the fact that CMT was our family's disease.

As for Sarah, she inherited the de Silva determination along with CMT. Although her symptoms constantly bother her and she has used some orthotics, she has not yet required surgery. Sarah became a notable sailor, with aspirations to compete in the Olympics. She was a sailing team captain at Northeastern and was known around Cape Cod as one the best sailors in the area. Sarah made it as far as the Junior World Championships, which in 2017 were in Enoshima, Japan. Then, for a number of reasons, Sarah decided it was time to put all her energies into her education and to sail recreationally rather than competitively.

Today, Sarah is an accomplished businesswoman and leader living in Boston. She has worked in several smaller entrepreneurial organizations in which her impact can most be felt. She is an excellent strategist, communicator, relationship builder and client manager. Sarah's longer-term goal is to be an entrepreneur and start and grow her own company. I am confident that she will do this at the right time and achieve much success.

Michelle and the girls have been the heart and soul of my life, even as our little family relocated multiple times as my career and history-making issues unfolded in the financial marketplace. For the timeline and context, keep reading.

Chapter 3

From Wheelbarrows to Wall Street: My Leadership Path

In December 1978, I started my first job as an usher at Cinema 140 in New Bedford, which was part of Lockwood/Friedman Film Corporation. A senior in high school, I was hired to help handle the Christmas season rush. The starting wage was $2.10 per hour. On both sides, we expected this to be a short-term job, ending right after the busy holiday season. As it turned out, Cinema 140 was a great company; business remained strong after the holiday season rush, and I continued to work there for years.

A few years into my time at Cinema 140, the owners temporarily closed the cinema to expand the complex from two to four screens. It looked like I was going to be out of a job for at least a few months. Willing to do whatever was necessary to earn some money, I asked the construction managers if I could work with their crew. After they were done laughing, the manager hired me to push around a wheelbarrow, picking up pieces of concrete and other construction materials. My job was to make sure the work environment was as clean as possible. It was heavy, grueling work, but I was glad to have the job.

One day, co-owner Roger Lockwood came to inspect the construction progress. He recognized me as one of the regular theater associates, now pushing a wheelbarrow. He stopped and asked what I was doing. I told him that I needed a job and had been hired by the construction team to help keep the place clean. Roger, who was my earliest leadership model and mentor, became a lifelong friend. He and I still laugh about that wheelbarrow encounter.

During college, I was promoted to manager of Cinema 140. Later, I was made manager of a second area theater complex. I was always eager to progress, and I needed to make money to pay for my college education. In the summer of 1984, I temporarily relocated to Ipswich to run the company's Strand Theatre. The manager had left, and we needed to prepare for the large crowds expected with the opening of the blockbuster film *Indiana Jones and the Temple of Doom*.

It was while I was working as manager at Cinema 140 that I fell ill and had to take time off to deal with my kidney issues. This led to my biggest takeaway from my time at the company: the correlation between treating associates well and a business's success. If you treat your associates as respected partners or colleagues, you are likely to have motivated and committed associates. Those associates, in turn, will treat your customers well. It creates a virtuous cycle.

Although I loved the company and leadership at Cinema 140, changes in the marketplace eventually led me to conclude it was time for a career change. On May 10, 1975, Sony introduced in Japan the LV-1901 console Betamax player, the first real comprehensive home entertainment system. And on August 23, 1977, the Victor Company of Japan (JVC), a competitor to Sony, introduced the VHS format in the US.

It took some time for these two formats to catch on, but by the mid-eighties, I became convinced that the cinema business was as good as dead. It might not disappear right away, but I did not intend to stick around and become a victim of a dying industry. After all, I reasoned, why would people pay good money to come to a movie theater when they could watch a movie from the comfort of their own homes for less money and aggravation?

An entire new industry was quickly growing as Blockbuster Video made it convenient to rent movies to play at home for a small fee. I often went to Blockbuster myself to pick up a few movies on a Friday night.

In the end, I was right about the challenges the industry would face but wrong about the pace and speed of those changes. It took Netflix, Hulu, Peacock, HBO Max, Disney+, and a global pandemic for that to occur. Meanwhile, I was nervous. It was time to make a move; it was time to take a big risk.

Once I was convinced that the cinema business was in trouble, I began looking for a job in an industry on a growth trajectory. In late 1986, I responded to a full-page ad in the *Boston Globe* for an entry level position at Fidelity Investments, the fast-growing Boston-based mutual fund company. Although I had no knowledge about the mutual fund business, I knew that the industry was growing rapidly and that Fidelity was successfully riding, and maybe even driving, the wave.

I was fortunate to receive an invitation to travel to Boston for an interview. The interviewer, however, explained that there was absolutely no reason for the company to hire me. I had no industry knowledge, no securities licenses, no deep leadership experience, and I lived over an hour away. As my hopes were deflating, the interviewer continued, "But there is something about you that I like. I see potential." He asked me if I wanted to be considered for Fidelity's management rotation program. Of course I did.

Individuals from many parts of the organization were involved in the interview process for the position. In total, I had approximately twenty interviews. One, while not memorable at the time, became important to me later on.

I started my career at Fidelity in February 1987. By December 1989, I was happily married to Michelle Garron, one of the original interviewers. I learned that Michelle was the only one in the group who had left the interview with a somewhat negative impression of me. In fact, she encouraged the company not to hire me. Michelle initially thought I was arrogant and didn't listen to her when she spoke; I still maintain that neither of these things was true.

Once I started at Fidelity, Michelle was initially distant. We often found ourselves in team meetings together, but we went our separate ways afterward—at least until we found ourselves in a securities exam prep course together.

At the outset of the course, we sat away from each other. Over time, I made sure to arrive early and leave an open seat beside me in case Michelle wanted to join me. One day, to my surprise, she sat in that open seat. This became a pattern.

One night after a company-sponsored event that we both attended, I got up the nerve to ask Michelle to dinner. Again, to my surprise and delight, she said yes. We had a great dinner that evening. All in all, it took me almost twenty-four months to convince Michelle that she had been wrong about her first impressions of me. This is one of the many situations where patience and persistence paid off.

I spent seventeen years at Fidelity Investments, in positions of increasing size, scale, and responsibility, ending my career there as senior vice president of brokerage operations. I was fortunate to have great mentors from a wide swath of the company's leadership. Whether I worked directly for these individuals or not, each helped shape me as a leader and as a person. My mosaic was growing and evolving at a fast clip. I'm deeply grateful for the lessons I learned, and the relationships I built at Fidelity.

During my years at the company, I learned how corporate culture shapes business and lays the framework for how a company goes to market and treats its clients. Fidelity was a family business, with Ned Johnson firmly in charge during my tenure there. The company's culture is a direct reflection of Ned's personal vision, belief system, and ability to engage and enlist those around him in that vision. His was a culture of constant innovation, constant motion, uncompromising ethics and integrity, protecting the company's brand, investing for the long haul, and always doing what was right, even if that caused the company to take a hit.

As with any organization, there were some not-so-positive takeaways from Fidelity, too. The company had a revolving door of leaders and organizational structures. It became a spectator sport to see which executive leaders were in the good graces and which were out. In terms of maintaining continuity and focus, this constant change was challenging for those of us at the lower levels of the organization.

My observations of this phenomenon helped me come to appreciate that there is no such thing as a perfect organizational structure. It's a waste of time to keep looking for one. There are only alternative structures, each with their own strengths and weaknesses. The only way to make inherently flawed organizational structures work is by creating a compelling vision and purpose, a focused strategy, common goals, and a culture in which individuals will sacrifice self-interest for the good of the whole. This fact is intricately tied to several of my core principles. As such, I will address it again at relevant junctures.

In early 2004, after a wonderful run, I decided it was time to leave Fidelity. While I had grown considerably, made a strong contribution to the company, and enjoyed my time there, it became apparent that it was time to move on. My growth had slowed and the company was changing in ways I did not always agree with. The revolving door of leadership was also wearing me down. Over the course of seventeen years, I had twenty-one different roles and seventeen different bosses. I was tired, and it was time to try my hand at something else.

My next opportunity was the direct result of an enduring relationship I had built in prior years and was now coming to fruition. While working at Fidelity, I had been fortunate enough to meet the Kemper family of UMB Financial Corporation out of Kansas City, Missouri. Fidelity and UMB had struck up a strong, mutually beneficial business relationship in the early- to mid-nineties, and I had the good fortune to play a role in developing and maintaining that relationship on behalf of Fidelity.

One time, when there was a rough patch in the relationship, my boss at Fidelity sent me to Kansas City to deliver a stern warning to UMB executives. While UMB had generally performed well over the course of the relationship, there was a period when their quality, timely processing, and technology had slipped to such a level that Fidelity's customers were experiencing serious service issues that Fidelity could not tolerate. The relationship between the two companies was at risk.

Banker and philanthropist R. Crosby Kemper Jr. was a fourth-generation industry leader and an icon in the business. Imagine me, a junior executive, sitting in the UMB headquarters building, talking to Crosby Kemper Jr. and his team about the company's performance. I had an important message to relay. I also had an opportunity to deepen my relationship with Crosby Jr. and his son, Sandy Kemper. Although the two could not have liked the message I delivered, I believe they respected the way in which I communicated with them.

I vividly remember sitting in the company's sixth floor, lavishly appointed executive dining room looking across downtown Kansas City. I was explaining to David Kling, UMB's head of operations, that the company's performance was considerably below par and that we were considering severing the relationship, which was one of UMB's largest and most profitable.

Later that afternoon, I sat on the couch in Crosby Jr.'s palatial office with a fireplace on one end and original artwork by the likes of Georgia O'Keeffe, Thomas Hart Benton, and Wayne Thiebaud all around me. I was intimidated as we discussed the economy, Federal Reserve policy, and other matters of the day. Crosby and I got into our conversation so deeply that I almost missed my flight back to Boston.

Over the next few years, my personal relationship with Crosby Jr. and Sandy Kemper continued to flourish. Michelle and I lived on Cape Cod, where the Kempers happened to have a summer home. We started having dinners together there each summer.

Imagine my surprise when, over one of our summer dinners, Crosby asked me to consider relocating to Kansas City to help lead UMB. Initially, I had no interest whatsoever. It took a few more years of dinners and conversations before I would entertain the idea.

Even then, I had some concerns about going to UMB. Although it was a public company, it was largely run by the Kemper family. The company had gone through numerous outside senior leaders over time, and I was concerned that the same might happen to me. There was also the question about how much latitude I might have to make needed changes. I was also concerned about shifting industries from mutual funds and brokerage to banking, which I knew little about.

Something Crosby said eventually swayed me. "I don't need another banker; I have plenty of capable bankers. What I need is someone who can develop a new, more contemporary strategy and inspire our team so that this company can be around for another hundred years."

Crosby indicated that he knew that banking had changed over time, and he was unsure about how to respond to the changes. He thought that bringing in someone from another related industry, especially an industry that had been beating up the banks over the past decade, would be a strategic step. Crosby wanted a fresh perspective from someone outside the banking industry. That's just what I needed to hear.

Michelle was not as enthusiastic as I was about moving to Kansas City. I remember her saying, "When hell freezes over I'll move to Kansas City."

We had a good thing in Massachusetts with our families close by and a strong cohort of friends. Michelle knew that I was ready for a change, but Kansas City seemed distant and alien. After much discussion and debate, she agreed that it was in our family's best interest for me to take the position. Our girls were in elementary school, so we felt that if we were ever going to relocate, now was the time.

In January 2004, I joined UMB, where I spent the next twelve years as the company's president and COO. For most of that time, I was also chairman and CEO of UMB Bank and chairman of UMB Fund Services.

My tenure at UMB was during the 2008 global financial crisis, which turned out to be a highly challenging and rewarding time. In addition to the ordinary components of my job within the company, my role required that I stretch myself to become a strong, visible leader of the Kansas City civic community.

It was in Kansas City that I came to understand that my leadership could be leveraged to support positive social change in ways I had not previously realized. Within a short time, I was chairing the regional United Way campaign, the chamber of commerce, and a movement to make Kansas City America's most entrepreneurial city. I was also fundraising for a new downtown YMCA and engaged in other meaningful community-wide activities. Michelle, in addition to supporting my work in the community, was pursuing her own interests. She chose to work for the Greater Kansas City Community Foundation and join the boards of numerous nonprofit organizations, including Truman Medical Center Charitable Foundation, Starlight Theatre, and Metropolitan Organization to Counter Sexual Assault (MOCSA).

The twelve years I spent at UMB were great years, full of personal and professional growth. I developed a strong relationship with Crosby Jr., members of the Kemper family, the UMB board, and the broader Kansas City community. My relationship with Crosby meant a lot to me.

Crosby was a larger-than-life figure in banking, politics, and the art world. He was a principled leader who stuck to his beliefs, regardless of the consequences. He wrote a book called *Maverick from the Herd*, a title that perfectly captured the essence of the man.

When executive leadership positions shifted in ways I'll explain later in the book, my relationship blossomed with Crosby's third son, J. Mariner Kemper, who became UMB's CEO. We developed a strong, trusting bond and worked together closely for over a decade. Mariner and I established a new vision for the company, innovating and growing new businesses along the way. This included a health care savings ecosystem that is the fourth largest provider in the US today. We also took a sleepy bank trust department and built it into a $30-plus billion asset management firm called Scout Investments.

I had a number of enduring takeaways from my time at UMB. Like Ned Johnson at Fidelity, Crosby Kemper Jr. was a visionary with a set of strongly held values, beliefs, and principles. One of these was to always do the right thing, no matter the cost. He would often say, "It's more important to do what's right, than what's popular."

PERSONAL AND PROFESSIONAL TIMELINE

EDUCATION

June 1979 — Graduated Dartmouth High School (Dartmouth, MA)

May 1984 — Graduated University of Massachusetts, Dartmouth, BS Management, Graduated with High Distinction

PERSONAL

December 10, 1989 — Married Michelle Garron (Norwood, MA)

August 5, 1993 — Daughter Christine born (Boston, MA)

March 8, 1996 — Daughter Sarah born (Cincinnati, OH)

PROFESSIONAL

December 1979 – January 1987
Lockwood/Friedman Film Corporation
Manager Cinema 140 (New Bedford, MA)

February 1987 – December 2003
Fidelity Investments
Senior Vice President, Vice President, Director, Management Trainee
(Boston, MA, Merrimack, NH, Covington, KY)

January 2004 – January 2016
UMB Financial Corporation (NASDAQ UMBF)
President UMB Financial Corporation,
Chairman and CEO UMB Bank, Chairman UMB Fund Services;
UMB Financial Corporation Board Member (Kansas City, MO)

February 2016 – August 2017
Scottrade Financial Services
President – Scottrade Financial Services,
President – Scottrade Investment Management,
President – Scottrade, Inc., Board Member (St. Louis, MO)

September 2017 – December 2020
TD Ameritrade, Inc. (NASDAQ AMTD)
Retail, President – TD Ameritrade, Inc. (St. Louis, MO)

January 2021 – May 2022
Harvard University Advanced Leadership Initiative (ALI)
Senior Fellow (Cambridge, MA)

While other companies in the financial industry were making decisions based on what was legal, UMB was making decisions based on what was *right*. To put it another way, we were guided by principles rather than managed by a prescribed set of rules. We adopted a belief that just because you can do something, does not mean that you should. This philosophy carried us through the Great Recession in fine form. I'll have a lot more to say about that later.

As is to be expected at any company, not all my experiences at UMB were positive. After the passing of Crosby Kemper Jr. in January of 2014, my relationship with Mariner Kemper began to change. He began excluding me from meetings and reducing my areas of responsibility. Although painful to receive, the message was clear: Mariner did not need or want me to continue to do the work I had been doing for the prior eleven years.

In late 2015, I received a call about an opportunity to become the president of Scottrade Financial Services and Scottrade Investment Management, located in St. Louis, Missouri. Scottrade was one of the premier online discount brokerage brands in the US, with millions of clients, and more than five hundred branches across forty-eight states. The company had an excellent reputation for client service delivery and advanced trading technology.

I was excited to join the company and did so in February 2016. I learned and grew during my time at Scottrade. Working closely with Rodger Riney—owner and one of the brokerage industry's titans—was a highlight of my professional career.

Rodger was a classic entrepreneur, and he challenged each of his leaders to operate the same way. He never wanted the company to get too big or too corporate. As the company grew to over $200 billion in client assets and toward $1 billion in revenue, Rodger always implored us to think like a big company but act like a small one.

Rodger's foundational principles included the golden rule of treating people as you would want to be treated, behaving as if your business is local even if it is primarily a digital business, and operating with a sense of urgency. Rodger was also comfortable taking measured risks—as long as there was a strong plan in place and sound risk management.

In the summer of 2016, my first year with the company, it became apparent that the best course for the firm would be a merger with a larger firm. Since the 2008 financial crisis, the brokerage industry had been coming under increasing pressure from perpetually low interest rates, the need for massive scale, and falling trading commissions. Some analysts were beginning to suggest that commissions might be headed to zero.

In this environment, scale became increasingly critical. Because of these pressures, along with our relatively small size and the fact that Rodger had recently been diagnosed with multiple myeloma, Rodger decided to sell the company to TD Ameritrade. We hired Goldman Sachs to help us with the sale, which was completed that fall.

In chapter 1, I touched on the story of how Tim Hockey, CEO of TD Ameritrade, unexpectedly invited me to join the TD Ameritrade Senior Operating Committee as president of the retail client segment. The role included oversight of product development, client experience, digital platforms, and investment management. This was by far the biggest and, in many ways, the most complex role I had taken on to date. It was a challenging period; I had to learn and assimilate into a new culture, manage a large integration, and find ways to jump-start growth. On many days, I wondered if that was what I really wanted to be doing at that point in my life.

I ended up loving the people and the position. We made some tremendous progress reframing and resetting the strategy, significantly improving the client experience, growing the business, and reinvigorating the nearly five thousand retail associates. The personal and professional growth and learning continued unabated.

At TD Ameritrade, I learned more about operating with a sense of purpose and urgency, working effectively in a horizontal fashion, and using all the available facts and data to make sound business decisions. Tim was by far the most data-driven leader I had ever worked for. While that was mostly a good thing, at times it seemed to slow us down and result in a lot of busywork. Sometimes you have to know when you have enough information to make a decision and then make it, knowing full well that if you are wrong, you can quickly correct course.

Somewhat surprisingly, two years after I took on this role, the decision was made to sell TD Ameritrade to Charles Schwab. The decision to sell was due to many of the same challenges that led to the Scottrade sale. Even though we were a $1.5 trillion organization with excellent trading technology, we felt the pressures from being small relative to Fidelity, Charles Schwab, Merrill Lynch, and the other larger brokerage firms and banks. By this time, Charles Schwab had already led the way to take trading commissions to zero, putting even more pressure on the smaller industry participants.

Once the deal was closed in the fall of 2020, I was severed by Charles Schwab and signed a two-year noncompete agreement. Participation in the ALI fellowship at Harvard, one of the most prestigious universities in America, seemed a fitting capstone to a career that had largely been about my own personal and professional growth and development while supporting the growth and development of others around me.

I started my career working as an usher, concession worker, and manager in movie theaters in New Bedford and Fall River, Massachusetts. As I was writing this book, I completed the ALI at Harvard University. I had an inferiority complex throughout most of my life—whether it was due to my CMT or my middle-class upbringing—and I never thought I would be worthy to attend such a prestigious university.

Today, I serve on numerous corporate and nonprofit boards, and as a mentor to many individuals. I am humbled and proud of these accomplishments. Still, I'm not done learning or making contributions. My mosaic is still developing. I know that I have much more to give as I successfully traverse my life's third chapter.

Chapter 4

Learning, Stretching, and Making My Way: Fidelity Investments

The offer came out of nowhere. I was an operations and customer service vice president based at Fidelity Investment's company headquarters in Boston. As such, I was keenly aware of the rapidly growing problems surrounding quality, operations, and service delivery at the company's gleaming new operations and customer service center in Covington, Kentucky. Performance had fallen to the point that clients were complaining loudly, their concerns now reaching the highest echelons of company leadership.

Transactions and service requests were delayed, processed incorrectly or incompletely, and sometimes not processed at all. Concerns were growing in the C-suite that legal claims, significant reputational damage, and regulatory scrutiny would soon be in the offing. Something had to be done—quickly. I definitely hadn't expected to be the one tasked with leading the turnaround that was to come.

When I began my career at Fidelity in 1987, I never imagined I would be as successful there as I turned out to be. I hadn't gone to an Ivy League school, and I joined Fidelity without any experience related to financial services. I began as a management trainee in an eighteen-month rotational program.

One day, about twelve months into the eighteen-month program, I approached the program executive, David Bourassa, and told him that I was seriously considering leaving the company. The program was not well organized and was moving too slowly for me. At one point, I spent an entire week alone in a conference room, reading the Investment Company Act of 1940 and the Securities and Exchange Act of 1933. This was not my idea of a good time or of accelerated learning. I had a sense of urgency about my career, and it seemed like Fidelity did not share that same urgency.

David understood and offered me thirty days to find a job on my own somewhere within Fidelity; otherwise, I would be dismissed from the program and the organization. It began to look like the risk I took in coming to Fidelity might have been a mistake.

Over the next few weeks, I was able to source two potential internal roles. One was in institutional sales, which was a fairly new and fast-growing part of the company. The other was in an area called mutual fund transfer agency operations. Both roles had merits. However, I thought that if I understood the company from the inside out (from the back-office operations out to sales versus the other way around), I would be more valuable to the organization over time.

I chose the role in transfer agency operations as a manager of mutual fund reconciliations. I hadn't envisioned myself doing that sort of work, but it was a start, which was all I wanted. I believed I could chart my own career from there. Education, hard work, and some prudent risk-taking had gotten me to this point, but I knew that my experiences and performance would be the elements to get me ahead. This role would have me managing people again, which I had done successfully as the manager of Cinema 140. I considered managing people an emerging strength for me.

As it turned out, this first position at Fidelity was exactly right for me. The role allowed me to learn a new part of the business while enabling me to grow as a leader. The management trainee program was an aberration; Fidelity otherwise did an excellent job of developing its management and leadership talent through a combination of licensing, formal classroom training, mentoring, and external programming. Under the circumstances, I felt like I had landed in a great first spot. Now it was up to me to take full advantage of the opportunity in front of me.

Things were going well when my boss, Paul Murphy, told me that I would be adding the bank account reconciliations department to my responsibilities. At first, I was apprehensive. What did I know about banking? I barely knew anything about reconciliations.

I quickly realized that this would be the first of many stretch assignments for me. Each assignment would add to my skills, knowledge, and abilities. This added role would be a good test of my stated desire to migrate away from a reliance on purely technical skills. It would require me to learn how to work successfully through others and trust them to do their jobs while I retained overall accountability. At this juncture in my career, I still found that a difficult proposition.

In the cinema industry, it was customary for the manager to work the concession stand, sell tickets, usher, and do the other tasks needed to run the business alongside the other employees. While I managed the employees, I also did the actual work.

I had always believed in the notion that *doing the work* was part of the way to gain credibility and respect from your team. I was a devotee of the adage, "Never ask someone to do something that you would not do yourself." That adage would not be fully applicable in this role.

Shortly after I took over bank account reconciliations, a top-performing employee came to see me. Diane "Dee" Robinson approached me, flustered. I could see that she was concerned about something but was reluctant to talk openly about it. I assured Dee that I would protect her, whatever she had to say. Dee nervously explained that our bank settlement accounts with the IRS were significantly out of balance; in fact, they had been that way long before I had become the group's manager.

Former managers had told Dee not to worry about the issue and to carry the item as an "exception to be resolved" on her reconciliations. Given that the unreconciled item was more than $10 million, Dee was becoming increasingly uncomfortable with this approach.

Since the problem item had been created even before Dee's watch, she wasn't sure what to do about it. Dee was not even certain if Fidelity owed money to the IRS or if the IRS owed money to Fidelity. The books were a mess, and she was seeking my counsel.

I hadn't the foggiest idea where to begin, but I told Dee that we would figure it out together. I assembled my entire team and told them that we would need to get to the bottom of this issue, and quickly. I assured them there would be no assessing of blame. No one would be fired. We just needed to get the matter resolved.

Not knowing the technical side of bank reconciliations, I established a timeline and a resolution roadmap, then relied on my team to sort through the books and records to determine the source of the issue and propose a way forward. I kept my boss informed throughout.

Over next few weeks, the team researched the issue from all conceivable angles, even pulling old information from storage boxes and microfilm archives. I brought in experts from outside the department to assist in unraveling the mystery. Eventually, the team and I became convinced that we had accumulated enough evidence to substantiate that the error was made by the IRS. We had assembled thousands of documents, knowing we would need detailed evidence if we had any chance of a recovery. The IRS owed Fidelity a substantial amount of money for a previous series of mistaken overpayments. Now we had to convince the IRS of *its* mistake.

As you might imagine, the discussions with the IRS were intense, complicated, and went on for months. After much back and forth, a few visits to the IRS's Andover Service Center, and hemming and hawing, the IRS eventually agreed with our analysis and issued Fidelity a refund check for more than $3 million.

The refund was obviously a big win, and I was proud of it. A source of greater pride, however, was the way the team persevered through some difficult research so that we were able to make a persuasive case to the IRS. Executives at Fidelity were also very pleased. A few weeks after the matter was finally resolved, I received a one-time spot bonus check for a significant sum to acknowledge my contribution to the accomplishment.

This situation reinforced my commitment to investigate and act when complex problems present themselves. One of my long-standing principles is to operate with a sense of urgency. Doing something is almost always better than doing nothing. This episode reinforced my principle. Good leaders do not let important matters lie fallow just because they are hard or complex. They face the realities of each situation head-on and do the right thing.

This episode also demonstrated to me the power of delegating, building a plan, relying on others, being determined to solve a problem, and persuasively presenting your case with incontrovertible facts. I learned valuable lessons about asking questions and digging deeper when something just does not smell right. I've often said to my later teams that "facts and data always win the day with me." This would become an essential underpinning of my leadership style.

Ultimately, I came to understand that leadership skills trump technical skills routinely, at least in a business context. This is not to say that a leader can ignore the details of an area he or she leads. The trick is to hire the best people, be humble enough to admit what you don't know, surround yourself with a complementary cast, have the ability to ask good questions, build strong metrics and reporting, and most important, trust those who have the deepest and broadest knowledge.

As I look back on this episode, I know that I failed in at least one important way. While I had overseen the research and resolution process, I had done little of the truly hard work of unbundling the incorrect accounting. While I worked the same hours as my team and supported them every step of the way, it was the team that untangled the mystery, not me. It did not even cross my mind to share some of my unexpected bonus with the team. I was just excited to tell Michelle. How selfish and shortsighted of me.

I had thanked the team and had undertaken other forms of public and private recognition, but I should have advocated for them to also receive monetary recognition for a job well done, or I should at least have shared a portion of my reward. I didn't do that, and when I realized it, I felt awful. I vowed to never make that mistake again.

The idea to build a new state-of-the-art operations and client service center in Covington, Kentucky came straight from CEO Ned Johnson, who was a visionary in every sense of the word. His vision for this facility was part of a broader strategy to geographically diversify away from the company's historic reliance on the city of Boston specifically, and Massachusetts more generally, as the primary place of employment for the company's thousands of employees. The company was growing rapidly and needed to diversify outside its historical boundaries.

Additional goals included building a new campus to Fidelity's specifications on a greenfield site, accessing lower labor costs in the Midwest, securing tax incentives in exchange for jobs, and introducing new processes and technologies without the resistance that often comes from individuals who are accustomed to doing things one way.

In 1992, the new center opened to great fanfare. It quickly became the pride of Fidelity and the centerpiece of the company's growing operations and customer service capabilities. The center included several leading-edge (some might say bleeding-edge) innovations, such as the introduction of image-based processing coupled with intelligent workflow routing. All customer mail would be centrally received, automatically opened, scanned, imaged, and transmitted to waiting associates anywhere across the country for processing. There would also be state-of-the-art check processing capabilities and a centralized inbound-outbound mail processing center.

The purpose was to enable a level of vertical integration and scale that could not be achieved with multiple remote sites. Image processing, coupled with enterprise workflow capabilities, would allow the processing to be done from virtually anywhere. The concept was great. The execution would prove challenging, given that all this had to be accomplished long before the advent of the internet and cloud computing.

Almost immediately after the site opened, problems began. In many ways, these problems might have been anticipated. A heap of brand-new technology was deployed; hundreds of new hires were receiving training at a new remote site; and the associates were being led by new leadership not yet fully accustomed to the "Fidelity Way." The early results included significant quality problems, delays, lost documents, and substantial client and associate frustration. The organization, however, could not allow this endeavor to fail. There was no going back.

My boss, Fred Knapp, based in Boston, had overall responsibility for the new operations center in Covington. As reports of problems at the new site came in, and although I had responsibilities for some functions at Covington, it never entered my mind that Fred might see me as the one with the leadership skills, business knowledge, cultural understanding, and capabilities to help turn around such a crucial operation.

In my mind, and I suspect in the minds of many others, I was still young and unproven, and in this situation, failure was not an option. But there Fred was in my office, asking me to uproot my family and move from my beloved Boston to Northern Kentucky. He sweetened the offer with a promotion to senior vice president, a sizable bump in pay, and a commitment to limit my time in Kentucky to two years, or until the bulk of the issues were demonstrably resolved.

The Covington assignment represented an opportunity to lead a crucial turnaround and demonstrate to Fidelity's leadership that I had what it took to grow into a significant senior leader. In addition to the calculation around the work side of things, however, there was the personal side to contend with. This would be the first of many key decisions that Michelle and I would need to contend with jointly as our careers and family life became more complex and intertwined. Something would need to give.

Michelle and I had been married just a few years when this opportunity arose. We had concluded earlier that we did not want to have all our employment eggs in one basket at Fidelity. We had seen many "Fidelity families" shattered after the 1987 and 1989 market crashes and subsequent painful but necessary staff reductions. It was gut-wrenching when one of two family members was let go, and even more so when both were severed.

Michelle had found an exceptional opportunity at Thomson Reuters (formerly Thomson Financial Services) as a leader on the development of their portfolio accounting system, PORTIA. While we were still in the same general industry, we were more comfortable that we had diversified our family's financial risk.

At the time the Covington opportunity arose, things were going well for Michelle at Thomson, and she was getting regular promotions. Michelle was also pregnant with our second child.

Together, Michelle and I analyzed the opportunity from every conceivable angle. We looked at the risks and the benefits, including what it would be like to live away from family and friends. I was especially concerned because my father was in poor health at the time.

In the end, we concluded the timing was not right. Although we knew that this might be shortsighted, we could not come up with a compelling reason to disrupt our lives at this juncture. We decided to take a pass.

The next day, I informed Fred that I was declining the role. While he was initially supportive, he clearly thought it was a big mistake. By Fred's way of thinking, taking this risk would allow me to grow more quickly and develop my leadership skills more thoroughly than staying at my current job.

A few weeks later, Fred returned to my office and closed the door. The situation in Covington had deteriorated further, with increasing client, associate, vendor, and internal business partner complaints. The individual currently leading the site, a recent hire from Merrill Lynch, was struggling to adapt to the Fidelity culture and Fidelity's rapid adoption of emerging technologies. He also lacked the deep partner relationships back in Boston that were needed to help him construct a viable turnaround plan.

This time around, Fred did not mince words. He made it abundantly clear that taking on this critical role and moving to Covington was no longer really an option for me. While Fred never said it directly, I suspected then that my career would flatline, or possibly even regress, if I did not take the position. After discussing it further, Michelle and I jointly concluded that this move was in our family's long-term best interest. It was off to Northern Kentucky for the de Silvas.

As the reality began to sink in that I would be taking on this assignment, I began to think about the many positive aspects of this opportunity. While there was always the risk of failure, I chose to focus on the impact of success.

Research over many years indicates that a tight correlation exists between the distance at which one operates away from corporate headquarters and one's professional growth, effectiveness, and job satisfaction. The greater the distance away from "corporate," the more satisfied the person tends to be in his or her work.

Working in a location away from headquarters provides more freedom to act independently, outside the glare that often happens at HQ, and to be removed from the politics and backbiting that tends to occur. Getting away from corporate to spread your wings is generally viewed as a healthy thing that accelerates personal growth and development. For this reason, many companies insist that leaders take on regional leadership assignments. This was to be my chance.

Because Michelle was pregnant with Sarah and still working, I lived alone in Kentucky for the first six months, flying back and forth to Boston most weekends. It took us that long to get our Massachusetts home sold, secure our desired housing in Northern Kentucky, and get our personal goods relocated. This was a challenging time for our small but growing nuclear family.

Michelle had decided that she would leave her job at Thomson as part of the move to Kentucky. The internet had not yet caught on, so working remotely wasn't an option. Although Michelle struggled with the idea of pausing her career, she decided to take on the role of stay-at-home mom at this point for the good of the family. It was a big sacrifice for her to make, and I never took it for granted.

As I traveled and spent more time in Covington, I found it extremely difficult to be away from Michelle and our toddler, Christine, whom I adored. Every day brought something new with our growing girl. Meanwhile, Michelle was experiencing a difficult time herself. She had resigned from her job months before it was time for her and Christine to move, and it was the dark of winter. She felt adrift without her professional identity. I supported Michelle as best I could from Covington while she was selling the house and preparing for the move.

On each of my trips, I searched in the airport for something to bring to Christine. One time, I found a collection of plastic ducklings based on *Make Way for Ducklings* by Robert McCloskey. I had read that book to my daughter multiple times. The story takes place in the Boston Public Garden, making it a favorite.

I brought Christine one of the eight plastic ducklings each time I came home until the collection was complete. We had a lot of fun with that as she waited in anticipation for the next member of her collection each week. The collection of Mrs. Mallard, Jack, Kack, Lack, Mack, Nack, Ouack, Pack and Quack stayed on Christine's bedroom shelf throughout her childhood. If ever a daughter had her father wrapped around her little finger, it was Christine.

Professionally, the Covington assignment was my most challenging thus far. One example shows just how bad things had become. Early in my tenure, on a Friday afternoon, I received a fax from our Cincinnati-based regional bank, informing me that they were about to fire us. I was alarmed and perplexed. How could this be?

It is not often that a vendor fires a large marquee client like Fidelity Investments without first speaking leader to leader. The fax stated that our quality, processing accuracy, and timeliness were so poor that we were creating untenable business risks for the bank. They provided multiple examples of processing, communication, and reconciliation issues. They gave us thirty days to cease all processing and deposit activity, close our accounts, and transfer all activity to another bank. This was all before the full digitization of check deposit activity.

The situation quickly became a crisis, but I also saw it as an opportunity. If we could bring the team and other parts of the Fidelity organization together and accomplish a critical outcome when we collaborated in a common cause, we would build our credibility within the organization. I saw this as a situation in which we could stage a turnaround in confidence and internal perception and quickly infuse the Fidelity culture into the newly opened Covington site. I resolved that we would make sweet-tasting lemonade out of lemons.

Leaving a depository institution is not a trivial undertaking. Upon receipt of the fax, I immediately reached out to Fred to discuss the situation. We needed to quickly find a bank that understood that our check deposit sizes would be significantly larger than most of their other retail depositors, which could expose them to more risk. They also needed to understand that our client service standards would ultimately be higher than most. There were few banks of sufficient size and scale in or adjacent to the Cincinnati market to adequately handle our business. Unfortunately, given the time pressures, we were not negotiating from a position of strength.

A few days later, I traveled, along with a few other Fidelity leaders, to the incumbent bank's offices in downtown Cincinnati. We wanted to negotiate an extended departure window. Upon arrival, we were quickly ushered into one of the largest conference rooms I have ever been in. There was no offer of coffee, water, soda, or anything else. We sat quietly and waited for the bank team to arrive.

Three bank executives came in and proceeded to sit at the farthest other end of the table. They did not shake our hands or engage in any small talk. I quickly realized that this meeting was not going to go well.

The most senior officer stated the bank's grievances and reiterated their position that we needed to be gone in thirty days. I said in a professional but firm manner that the proposed arrangement was entirely impractical and would create additional risks for both organizations. After additional discussion they eventually conceded to a ninety-day departure window. The meeting lasted a total of ten minutes.

Even at ninety days, this was a tall order, but we had to execute on it—and execute well. I knew that if we completed the transition quickly and successfully, it would be the beginning of a new day for the Covington team and the broader Fidelity organization.

Prior leadership had run the Covington operation as an island with the prevailing view that as the new shiny object, we did not need any help. Knowing the Fidelity culture as I did, I knew this was a mistake. I quickly reattached the organization to the mainland, assembling a top-notch team of almost fifty people from technology, product management, legal, risk, compliance, marketing, and many other parts of the Fidelity enterprise. This was the first time that the Covington team truly reached back with humility to the Boston teams for support.

For the next ninety days, the teams collaborated while we built a comprehensive conversion plan, interviewed, selected, and negotiated agreements with a new bank, built the conversion routines, and proactively communicated with customers, vendors, and associates. We also worked internally to rapidly improve our processing quality, timeliness, and communications to ensure that the new relationship would get off on the right foot. It was Fidelity's concept of continuous improvement at its best.

In the end, we left the incumbent bank within the allotted window and successfully migrated our business to another more accommodating provider. This institution turned out to be a much more flexible, nimble, innovative, and supportive partner. We communicated clearly with our new partner the exact specifications and performance standards we expected. They did the same with us. We were clear with our own teams as to our commitments in terms of quality, accuracy, and timeliness (something we called QAT). It was no longer us against the bank. It became us *with* them, guided by a superior client experience as our collective North Star.

After all the planning, the conversion went off without a hitch. Hard work and persistence paid off. We made lemonade out of lemons.

The sense of pride within the team was palpable. Team members came to realize that they had succeeded by working together in an unselfish fashion. Each had taken responsibility for his or her respective component while recognizing that the entire conversion would be successful only if all components were executed flawlessly.

The team's work on this conversion stretched beyond the average corporate teamwork. It was true collaboration. The new cross-company relationships that were created in the process were a great benefit. The relationships that were forged out of crisis would serve us well on the difficult road ahead.

Over the next two years, there were many ups and downs, but my team and I eventually turned the operation around. Every one of our key metrics improved considerably, including customer satisfaction, associate satisfaction, and operational quality. Another important outcome was that internal business partners stopped complaining about "Covington." Our team had demonstrated that the decision to build a major regional site there had not been a mistake. It was nice to be off the corporate front page.

During most of the two years I was there, Fred came to Covington regularly, often weekly, to check on the progress of the turnaround. We sometimes met while he was in town, but he often came in for a day or two and interacted sparingly with me and the team. Fred was there if I wanted or needed him, but he did not micromanage me in any way. I found it odd that he would spend the time traveling and then interact sparingly with the team, but that was okay with me. I guessed he felt that we were generally on the right track.

After two years, we had made enough progress that Fred was able to hold up his end of his bargain. It was time for me and my family to head back to Boston. I reached this milestone with mixed emotions, knowing that I had grown quite a bit on this assignment. I had also enjoyed the freedom and independence that came with being away from headquarters.

That said, I was extremely proud of the work I had done in Covington, and I looked forward to returning to my native Boston for even bigger challenges. It was good to be going home. I thought Michelle would be excited to be returning home; instead, she was not. For her, this meant that the family was being uprooted again—after only a short eighteen months. She was just beginning to establish some good friendships in Covington when we were transferred back to Boston.

One night back in Boston, at a cocktail party attended by some of the company's most senior executives, I had a confusing and troubling interaction with Mark Peterson, one of the company's top executives. I had met Mark on numerous occasions and had made presentations before him a few other times as well. Mark was a smart and insightful leader for whom I had great respect.

During our conversation, Mark let me know how pleased and proud he and the Fidelity executive team were of me and the good work that my team and I had done turning around the Covington operation. Then he let it slip that some of the members of the executive committee were a bit surprised that I succeeded in the way I did. Some of the Fidelity executives had been unsure that I had yet developed the business maturity, gravitas, and overall leadership skills needed to take on such an important and visible challenge.

I, of course, listened politely to Mark and thanked him for his confidence and support. However, I left that cocktail party perplexed and upset. What was Mark trying to say? Did the executive team have confidence in me when I went to Covington or not? Were they really pleased with the outcome? Had I been set up somehow? I needed to find out.

After a restless night, I went to see Fred bright and early the next day. This time I was the one to gently close his door. When I told him about my encounter with Mark the night before, Fred just brushed it off. Not satisfied, I pressed for more. Fred kept saying that there was nothing to be concerned about. I had enjoyed success in Covington, and all was well with the Fidelity executive leadership team. I believed he was right about that, but I knew that there was some deeper reality.

Finally, it all became clear to me. The reason Fred traveled to Covington so often during my time there was to give the executive committee confidence that he was on the ground backstopping me. Fred had told me time and again that he had the confidence that I could do the job, so it wasn't about that. His visits were to provide comfort to the executive committee that he was on top of the situation and would be on hand in the event that things started to go awry. He was the one with the seasoning and business savvy. I was the one with the energy and the desire to prove myself.

Given that Fred had backed the idea for me to take the Covington job to the Fidelity Executive Committee, he clearly had a vested self-interest in my success. If I failed, it would reflect poorly on him. But more than that, I came to realize that Fred was taking a risk on me, pushing me hard, exhorting me onward, and simultaneously protecting me, thereby rapidly accelerating my personal and professional development. He was providing the support necessary to ensure that I succeeded without interfering and stunting my growth.

By coming to Covington and always remaining available to me, Fred had built what I've come to think of as a fence around me. In this context, the imagery suggests to me freedom, with security, in a specific area of responsibility. It's not a "fencing in" to restrict but an established area in which to spread an emerging leader's wings.

I liken this to the difference between a mustang that is allowed to roam free across the American West and a horse that has defined boundaries as designated by a fenced-in area. The mustang can roam wherever it wants, including into territory where predators might be a threat or to the edge of a cliff where the risk of falling off is a real possibility. Contrast that to the horse that has a large territory in which to roam free but with defined boundaries. That horse still has a large area in which to run free and explore, but it is protected by the presence of the fence.

When senior leaders provide emerging leaders with boundaries that are wide enough and the responsibilities are well defined, the individual and the organization win. The Pembroke Hill School in Kansas City, which my daughters attended, has the motto "Freedom with responsibility." That fits here as well.

In Covington, Fred was overseeing my critical actions and decisions but keeping his distance to allow me to make the important decisions. I am confident he might have done some things differently than I had if he was in charge, but that was not the point. The broader point was whether my chosen course of action was going to lead to a significant derailment. If not, Fred had the wisdom to let me continue my work. I've always been grateful for the way Fred treated me and allowed me to flourish and build my confidence as an emerging leader. This experience and the lessons it taught me are bright portions of my leadership mosaic.

Near Failure Is a Much Better Teacher Than Actual Failure

A key role of any enlightened, contemporary leader is to identify, develop, and nurture talent. Taking risks on individuals, especially younger, upwardly mobile leaders who hold promise, is crucial in this role.

Many say that failure is a great teacher. We know that Abraham Lincoln lost jobs, failed at business, was defeated in his bid for the state legislature, was defeated for Speaker, and was defeated for the Senate before enjoying his ultimate success as President. Michael Jordan was purportedly cut from his high school basketball team for "a lack of skill." J. K. Rowling was famously rejected by twelve publishers before *Harry Potter and the Philosopher's Stone* was successfully published.

In Silicon Valley, it is a badge of honor to fail, sometimes multiple times, before succeeding. The idea is that each failure adds to your understanding of what not to do the next time around.

The "if you don't succeed, try and try again" approach seems to work for some, but not for all, especially those who work inside larger public or private companies. While failure can be a great teacher, it can also destroy the confidence and upward mobility of individuals and teams.

My own experience is that *near failure* is often a better teacher than *actual* failure. Think of near failure as encompassing essentially all the critical lessons of actual failure without the emotional and psychological impacts on a person's confidence, reputation, and self-esteem.

A March 2021 article by Harvard Business School senior writer Kristen Senz titled "How to Learn from the Big Mistake You Almost Make," reminds us that there is much to be learned from near mistakes. Senz reports on a study conducted by Amy C. Edmondson, Olivia S. Jung, and colleagues who interviewed seventy-eight oncology radiologists to discover their level of willingness to report close calls with patients.

The study results show that those who have a higher level of perceived psychological safety are more likely to admit their close calls than those who do not. A leader's attitude and language surrounding near misses can make a big difference. Edmondson says, "People don't pay enough attention, especially in the business world, to the potential goldmine of near misses."

Effective leaders acknowledge that things go wrong and people who catch mistakes are demonstrating "vigilance and resilience." They are more likely to see their aspiring leaders grow faster and further from near failure. More often than not, it is better to create a pattern of learning from mistakes and near failure than to reach the point of actual failure.

Following the Covington assignment, I filled a number of roles at Fidelity. The company believed in frequently moving leaders into different positions. Stretch assignments with new teams and new areas of the business allowed me to grow substantially.

It was a remarkable run for someone who started with no industry experience, limited leadership experience, and no real idea what career path he would ultimately follow. I hadn't known if I would stay at Fidelity for six months or six years. I never imagined that I would stay for seventeen great years. I came to love the financial services industry and concluded long before leaving Fidelity that I would make a career in the industry.

Both my parents passed away during my time at Fidelity. My dad passed away in February 1994 and my mom passed away five years later in April 1999. I loved and respected them both, and I grieved for them.

Norman de Silva raised all four of his children in a loving but firm way. He was an uncompromising proponent of hard work and personal integrity. I remember him telling me, "You only have one reputation, so build it one brick at a time." He would remind us that reputations take a lifetime to build and just a moment to collapse. Dad was my first example of a principled person, a model of integrity. I admired my dad greatly.

Dad worked in the retail sector as a store manager. He earned a reputation for hard work, fair-mindedness, and a focus on taking care of the people who worked for him. He was also always focused on delivering excellent customer service. Dad frequently won corporate awards and was once recognized for his excellent work with an all-expenses-paid trip to Bermuda.

I remember visiting Dad at his store at various times. His employees frequently came up to him to thank him for something he had done for them. I think he innately understood the power of taking care of employees so that they could take care of customers. Perhaps I initially got the idea about the power of taking care of associates from observing Dad at work.

My father persevered through his CMT when it would have been easier to slow down. He would have none of that, even after losing a leg. I admired his tenacity. I intentionally added that characteristic to my mosaic.

I'm grateful to be able to say I had a father who was always there for me, no matter the situation, one who was always there to support me. I know that many people do not have that.

I'd always known Mom was a special person, active in her church, the Dartmouth Youth Athletic Association, the Dartmouth High School Band, and more. Mom's favorite thing as a registered nurse was being present at the arrival of new lives at St. Luke's Hospital. I've heard hundreds of stories about Mom's heroics in the delivery room, helping new mothers and fathers with the most precious event ever to happen to them.

An only child, Mom had a difficult childhood. Her family lived on a farm, and Mom was expected to be a full participant in taking care of things. My grandmother was particularly tough on her. Mom often remarked that it was her father who showed her the love and compassion she desperately needed. Her father's sudden death, from a heart attack in his sixties, was a shock and a source of deep grief for her.

Mom could be a bit of a character. She enjoyed having a good time, especially with her family. There was an abundance of parties and holidays to cook for and plenty of people to entertain.

If you have seen the movie *My Big Fat Greek Wedding*, you know that the bride's father believed Windex is the cure for anything—from poison ivy to psoriasis. In my mother's case, the magic cure was olive oil. I can't tell you how many times I drank straight olive oil, sometimes with a bit of garlic, to cure whatever was ailing me.

Like her father, my mom passed away unexpectedly during middle age. She was diagnosed with a brain tumor on a Friday and dead by Monday morning. I was grief-stricken.

Mom's funeral was a testament to her life of service, and it caught me by surprise. I stood in the receiving line as individuals—whom I did not know—expressed their sorrow. I marveled at the number of people who related stories of the impact my mother had on their lives at the time of their child's birth. A few even named a child after my mother because of something remarkable she had done.

Until her death, I had no idea that Mom had been instrumental in founding an organization called Parents Enduring Grief (PEG) to support parents who lost a child during childbirth. I knew Mom went out a few times each week to some group, but I did not have the details. She kept her service to others quiet, even from her family. After Mom's death, I met with the other nurses who helped to form this organization. We have tried to keep the program going on her behalf. Incidentally, my mom—Margaret—also went by Peg.

St. Luke's Hospital asked if the family would drive the funeral procession by the hospital so that those who could not leave work to attend Mom's funeral could pay their last respects. Imagine my surprise when we turned the corner and roughly one hundred of Mom's friends and colleagues lined the street to say goodbye. I was never so proud to be her son.

During the funeral service itself, the family participated in different ways. My sister sang, and my brothers and I eulogized her. A few days before, as I was preparing my remarks, I got to thinking about all that Mom had accomplished with her family, her work, her generosity, and her many friendships. It seemed that the best way to remember her was to think about the role she played at the start of so many lives. By my calculations, Peg de Silva had been present at approximately 10,000 births during her time working in the delivery room. I cannot think of a more moving tribute to her.

Mom's work on behalf of others, however, didn't end with her job. Her work gave her insight into a profound need in the community, and she stepped up to meet that need. Mom, matriarch of a humble Massachusetts family, co-founded an organization to relieve suffering. She was a true community leader. Eventually, I would realize that I, too, needed to be a community leader dedicated to relieving the suffering of others. As Mom's insights would lead her to champion a cause, so would mine—but not for a long time yet.

I studied many leaders during my years at Fidelity. I learned what to do—and what not to do— from them. I was physically close to some leaders while more remote from others. Learning by observation and incorporating those elements that I admired into my leadership style was an important part of my development. I built my mosaic by observation, practice, and experience.

I never worked closely with Ned Johnson, so he never knew the significant impact he had on my professional mosaic at an early and impressionable age. I studied his every move, read everything by him I could get my hands on, and listened to his every word. Over the course of the years, we did have a few phone calls and personal interactions. I learned something each time.

For example, one time Ned came to Covington to see how the turnaround was progressing. He wanted a tour of the operations and a demonstration of our new image processing and workflow management system.

I greeted him upon his arrival, and we, along with a few other members of my team, began the tour. VIP visits were always highly orchestrated affairs with tight schedules and stops in various parts of the organization. On this day, Ned would have none of it.

The first order of business was to conduct a demonstration of the image processing capability. We had serious issues with the production version and were planning to show Ned an updated, soon-to-be-released beta version in a conference room. Ned informed us that he just wanted to walk around the floor and stop at various employees' desks to see how things were really working. I was horrified.

Ned got to see all the issues the associates were facing, including long delays between items to be processed, screens that were far too small for the work at hand, and document images presented upside down, thus requiring additional steps and lost productivity. He was not pleased.

At one point, Ned looked at me and told me to move along, that he would take it from there. I figured that was the end of my career. It wasn't. Ned just wanted to be with the employees and get the unadulterated truth from them. He understood that the true knowledge was at the front line, not through a scripted managerial presentation. I took note of this and added this to my leadership style.

Ned was personally involved at a level that many CEOs might consider unnecessary. No detail was too small or unimportant. He carried a small pad in his jacket pocket that he was always writing notes on. He was a perfectionist who expected the same from his leadership team and associates. He continually pushed the organization to perform at higher and higher levels of excellence. At the same time, he was committed to integrity and ethics. For Ned Johnson, it was foundational to always do the right thing, even if it cost you in the short term. At the helm of a privately held company, he had the ability to take the long view of things.

> **Model of a Visionary Leader: Ned Johnson**
>
> One of the most important jobs of a CEO is to conceive, communicate, nurture, and protect the company's vision and culture. Culture, built over time, is the glue that holds organizations together through good times and bad. It is created and reinforced through consistent actions, not words. Ned Johnson was a master at engaging others in a compelling vision and rewarding a winning culture.
>
> Regarding vision, I'm frequently reminded of an old story. A man walks by a worker handling bricks. He asks the man, "What are you doing?"
>
> The man answers, "I'm laying bricks."
>
> The observer travels a little farther and encounters another worker handling bricks. Again, he asks, "What are you doing?"
>
> The man answers, "I'm building a wall."
>
> The observer travels yet a little father and encounters a third worker handling bricks: "What are you doing?"
>
> "I'm building a cathedral."
>
> Ned Johnson was the kind of leader who could engage Fidelity associates at all levels in building the equivalent of a financial services cathedral. Ned Johnson also had an uncanny ability to foresee macro changes long before others did. Where others were comfortable with the status quo, he saw opportunity. When others were zigging, Ned knew it was time to zag. Fidelity had been successful for quite some time because of Ned's willingness to disrupt himself, his firm, and the industry time and again. Not every initiative was a success, but Ned

certainly was right more than he was wrong, especially on the larger things. A few examples will illustrate this point.

In 1974, Ned Johnson had a simple but revolutionary proposition: He thought that if you made it easy for customers to withdraw funds, they would put more money in. While other firms made the process of withdrawing funds as difficult as possible in an attempt to retain their client's assets, Fidelity made it easy by introducing a simple check writing feature on its money market mutual funds. Ned was proven right. Once the ability to withdraw funds without friction was put in place, the funds came flowing in. A standard practice today, this was unheard of at the time.

Johnson also wondered why mutual fund pricing could only occur at the end of a trading day. This seemed outdated to him. He thought Fidelity could utilize technology to price mutual funds each hour of the trading day, allowing for intraday subscriptions and liquidations. If Fidelity could figure it out, it would be a game changer. Once again, he was challenging a well-established convention that no one else thought could or should be challenged.

Innovations are generally made by challenging existing conventions or creating new ones. Notwithstanding the extremely difficult task of placing a value on a basket of stocks, bonds, and other assets on an intraday basis, Ned was adamant that Fidelity figure out how to do this on a select group of mutual funds every hour during every market day.

From this, Fidelity created hourly pricing on the Select Funds to provide additional points of entry and exit for investors throughout the trading day. It was not like trading a stock, which could be done almost instantaneously, but it was a quantum leap forward for investors who wanted the opportunity to enter and exit the market on an intraday basis through a narrow basket of industry-specific stocks.

This family of approximately thirty-five mutual funds became popular with more active investors who were seeking intraday liquidity and more frequent trading options. As these funds were generally smaller, they also served as a wonderful training ground for up-and-coming fund managers. The Select Funds were the harbinger of the exchange traded fund (ETF) industry that has grown with so much success over the past ten years.

> Ned Johnson was also fanatical about leveraging technology to deliver superior customer service. Fidelity was one of the first firms to have touch-tone telephone service and trading, and a myriad of internet-enabled services when those capabilities came along. The company also invested significantly in advanced call routing and call management technologies to improve customer service delivery.
>
> Ned also believed in, and heavily promoted, the Japanese concept of *kaizen*. Kaizen refers to business activities that continuously improve all functions and involve all employees, from the CEO to the assembly line workers. In many ways it is comparable to Six Sigma, which provides organizations with the tools and techniques to improve their business processes. Continuous improvement was a way of life at Fidelity. It made a big difference and resulted in Fidelity having some of the best client satisfaction scores in the industry.
>
> Robert Kennedy once said, "Some men see things as they are, and say why. I dream of things that never were, and say why not." This describes Ned Johnson and his Fidelity culture.

One day, a little later in my career, I was sitting in my Boston office when the phone rang. My administrative assistant came in, saying, "Peter, Mr. Johnson is on the phone."

At the time, I was a member of the firm's middle management layer. Although I had met Ned Johnson on a few occasions, I did not know him well enough to expect an unannounced call from him, but there it was. My palms and forehead began to sweat as I wondered, What could he want from me? Am I in some kind of trouble?

While I wouldn't say Ned had a full-out temper, he was known for being direct and animated when upset. Once I found the courage to pick up the phone, Ned engaged in some short pleasantries. Then he asked, "Are you the one responsible for the bill payment product?"

While I had operational responsibility for the product, I was not the overall product manager. That said, I had learned earlier in my career that when someone above you is asking, it is not important to get into details about who "owned" the product. At least for the duration of this phone call, I owned it, no matter what the situation was.

With that established, Ned, in a loud and animated voice, said, "Our bill payment product is just awful. How could we develop such a lousy product and put it in front of our clients? It's an embarrassment."

I was scared to death. The worst possible scenario had occurred. Ned Johnson associated me with a product he vehemently disliked.

When I could get a word in edgewise, I made the huge mistake of trying to calm him down, saying, "We recognize that the product has some shortfalls. We are actually in the middle of considering a major upgrade to the product in near future, Mr. Johnson. We are currently negotiating with a number of prospective vendors, including Microsoft." My response sent Ned into a near rage.

"What?!" he barked. "Why are we even considering Microsoft for this product? Don't you know that Bill Gates is trying to take over the world?"

Obviously, the quality of the call was deteriorating quickly. I had no idea what to say. Fortunately, Ned soon ended the call. His final words to me were, "Please, just fix it!"

As I hung up, I once again guessed my career was about to end. The most powerful person in financial services had just called me and laid out in no uncertain terms what I needed to do—or else.

Common wisdom at Fidelity indicated that it was okay if Ned Johnson knew your name. And it was okay if he knew your face. But if he was able to put the face and the name together, it was the kiss of death! I felt sure I had just fallen into that category.

A few weeks later, the phone rang. Once again, my administrative assistant informed me that Mr. Johnson was on the phone. I asked, "What does his mood seem like?"

She said, "Mr. Johnson seems calm and pleasant."

I gingerly picked up the phone and greeted the chairman and CEO of the company. I quickly assessed that Ned was in a much better mood this time around. I decided to be quick on the draw and proceeded to tell him about all the progress we had made and things we had accomplished in the intervening period. I also let him know that we would not be using the Microsoft product.

This seemed to please him very much. He asked, "Did you know that recently someone in Europe threw a pie in Bill Gates' face?"

On the whole, Ned was extremely pleased with the progress. I felt the tension in my shoulders release. We proceeded to have a wonderful chat about his views on the state of the industry, some significant work going on at Fidelity, and other topics germane to the business.

What's the point of this story? It's that details are important, no matter how far you move up the ladder. I have seen many leaders who have no real clue about what goes on below them. I always wonder how those leaders lead without a firm understanding of how things really operate.

After seventeen years at Fidelity, I was proud of my accomplishments and grateful for what Ned Johnson and my other formal and informal mentors had instilled in me. Still, feeling that my growth was slowing down and weary of constantly changing roles and leaders, I knew it was time to move on.

When Crosby Kemper Jr., with whom I'd kept in touch for many years, including those summer dinners on the Cape, asked me to consider moving to Kansas City to help lead UMB, I was surprised. I was also ripe for the change. My career at Fidelity had seemingly peaked and it was time for a new challenge. Michelle, however, was not excited about moving to the Midwest. Eventually, we both concluded that taking this opportunity was in our family's best interest. Michelle and I packed our things and prepared for life in the Midwest. As we did, I had no idea of the seismic events that would shake the financial world during our tenure there.

Chapter 5

Growing Up as a Consequential Leader: UMB Financial Corporation

It was a normal Friday morning in April 2004, only a few months into my role as president and COO of UMB, and I was still learning the ropes. At around 10 a.m., I received a call from Crosby Kemper Jr.'s administrative assistant, asking me to report to the Kemper home. A matter had arisen that needed immediate attention. Nothing could have prepared me for what was about to unfold.

Crosby was one of America's great bankers from a highly respected family of bankers. His father, R. Crosby Kemper Sr., had started City National Bank in Kansas City, Missouri, in 1913. By the time I came on board, the company was a multibillion-dollar commercial and retail bank and a multifaceted financial services organization.

Crosby had earned a reputation for being smart, cautious, and shrewd. It was well known throughout the Midwest that he was a conservative banker who would only take calculated risks, ones in which the chance of loss was negligible. Crosby always kept "extra" capital, just in case. This was not uncommon for someone who came of age during the Great Depression. At one point, a rating agency declared UMB "one of America's strongest banks." Crosby liked the line so much he adopted it as part of UMB's brand messaging.

While Crosby's conservative approach slowed the growth of the company in relation to its competitors, it also kept the company more stable during difficult economic times. This cautious approach also extended to other parts of the organization, including the trust investments area.

When managing investments, a primary objective is to provide strong risk-adjusted returns to clients. For Crosby, it was never about absolute or even relative returns. From his point of view, the proper measurement was return *of* capital, not return *on* capital. This philosophy made it difficult for the investment team to outperform their respective indices.

Crosby consistently took the long view of his business and brand reputation. While UMB did not fully participate in the excesses in the economy and financial markets that occurred from time to time, neither did the company fully participate in the downside. This approach resulted in a steady—if not flashy—company with which Crosby was comfortable. He often reminded us that we should not take any action that would risk the franchise or taint the brand.

Crosby was known to be a bit impetuous, cantankerous, and difficult to work for. At six foot seven, with a full head of white hair, he was an imposing figure. His voice was deep and loud, and he spoke with confidence. You always heard Crosby long before you saw him. He often regaled us with stories about his life in business, politics, art, ranching, and the history of Kansas City. He served in the US Navy and was a respected member of the Greatest Generation. He was highly principled, strong willed, and not the best listener. Once his mind was made up about something, it was nearly impossible to move him off that position.

These traits often led to disagreements with senior company leadership. Unfortunately, this resulted in a revolving door of nonfamily leadership and even some turnover within the Kemper family. When I joined as the nonbanker, nonfamily member from Boston, the over/under bet was that I would not last a year. At least I proved them wrong about that.

When I joined UMB, Crosby Jr. had stepped back; he was in the process of slowly handing the leadership of the company to his eldest son, Crosby Kemper III (C-III), who was the company's current CEO and my boss.

When I arrived at the Kemper home, Crosby Jr. sat me down and informed me that C-III had unexpectedly resigned from the company, effective immediately. I was shocked. I had spent the previous day with C-III in Milwaukee, visiting one of our subsidiary companies, and all had seemed fine. C-III seemed in particularly good spirits the day prior.

I learned that C-III was not stepping down for health reasons, and there was no malfeasance suspected at the company. This was clearly a personal matter, and I didn't press for more details. As a public company, the CEO's resignation was clearly a business matter, but it was also a family matter, and I knew where to draw the line.

My reaction, as almost anyone's would be, was to first think about C-III and hope he was okay, next to think about the future of the company, then to think about how all this might affect me and my career. I never had the chance to speak to C-III at the time of his departure or thereafter. I regret that to this day.

UMB was a midsize bank, but due to its multiple other lines of nonbanking business and broad geographic footprint, it was a highly complex institution. Crosby Jr. had opted to complement his conservative lending style with other fee-producing businesses that came with less credit risk. This enabled the company to achieve strong returns without the volatility associated with risky lending. It was a smart approach.

C-III hadn't been the strongest executive leader. I sometimes thought he was in the role more out of family duty than his love of banking, leading people, and running complex organizations. He was an intellectual more than a leader. He had a difficult time making challenging decisions and could be unfocused at times. Despite his shortfalls as a business leader, C-III was an outstanding community leader and seemed to fully enjoy that part of his responsibilities. He was highly likeable, and others responded positively to his warmth and genuineness.

I had been hired, in part, because of C-III's lack of broad business acumen. Crosby Jr. had thought that C-III could best leverage his talents by focusing on his community work on behalf of the company, and that I, as president, could lead the internal parts of the organization. In the few months I had been in my role, the approach had been working, making it harder to understand why Crosby III was leaving.

After we finished the initial discussion about C-III's departure, my thoughts returned to what this might mean for me, my family, and my career. Given the history of the revolving door of leaders at UMB, Michelle and I had always been aware that accepting this job and moving to Kansas City came with risks. With this new development, the risk was now even higher.

I began to think we had made a terrible mistake. Michelle was still living in Boston. The house we had purchased when we returned to Boston from Covington had not yet sold, and our daughters were about to finish the fifth and second grades, respectively. I wasn't looking forward to explaining to Michelle what had happened, especially since I did not know all the circumstances myself.

I had all that yet to face, but more urgently, I needed to work with Crosby and the Kemper family to deal with the ramifications of C-III's unexpected departure on the company. We would need to address our board, investors, the Kansas City community, and more than two thousand employees on Monday. They would have questions, and we were going to need cogent answers. We quickly needed to develop and communicate a go-forward plan, one that inspired trust and confidence in the organization and its leadership.

Crosby Jr., his wife Bebe, sons Alexander (Sandy) and J. Mariner, and some board members spent the weekend discussing the merits of various leadership approaches. Ultimately, we came up with five options.

Option one. Put Crosby Jr. back in the CEO seat and let him run the company, as he had done successfully for many years, with me working by his side. While this would convey a sense of stability to the street, it might cause significant concern among the clients, community, and associates as to the company's willingness to change. Crosby was well into his seventies at this juncture, and the company's growth was already lagging behind its peers.

Option two. Bring Sandy Kemper back from his entrepreneurial venture to lead the organization. Sandy had previously been CEO of the company but left to start Perfect Commerce (aka eScout). While this might go over well in some quarters, Sandy's sudden departure a few years prior had left some wondering what had happened and whether he and his father were in alignment with respect to the company's direction.

Option three. Install me as CEO over the entire organization. (I had been with the company only four months at this point.) While I felt that I could succeed at this, I was still quite new to the UMB organization, the board, the community, and the Kemper family. Equally important, I did not have the Kemper last name, which was important to Crosby Jr. For almost a hundred years, the company had been led by a Kemper family member. It was not the right time for that tradition to change. I fully understood and appreciated that.

Option four. Install Mariner Kemper, Crosby's youngest son, as CEO. Mariner, aged twenty-nine, lived in Denver. He was chairman and CEO of the Colorado-based subsidiary, UMB Bank Colorado. Mariner was a good leader internally and in the Denver community, but he was inexperienced in leading a large, complex public company.

Option five. Sell the company. This option never gained a lot of traction, but as fiduciaries, management and the board needed to consider it. The Kemper family was fiercely independent and would find it difficult to give up the company, especially under these circumstances.

Each of the options had risks. There was a lot to consider, including the reactions of investors, analysts, competitors, associates, and the community. We did not want our stock to take a big hit once the announcement was made early the following week. We needed to project strength, not weaknesses, and a solid forward-looking approach. Otherwise, a competitor might try to make a hostile bid for the company during this period of uncertainty.

Whatever plan we announced also had to win over the hearts and minds of our associates or risk a flight of talent. We just had to get the plan and the messaging right.

At one point during the weekend, Crosby asked Mariner to fly to Kansas City to participate in the discussions in person. Even before he arrived, there was a general sense that asking Mariner to lead the organization as chairman and CEO of UMB Financial Corporation (the holding company) might be the best approach. Still, there was much to sort out.

When Mariner arrived on Sunday, Crosby Jr. asked the two of us to spend time discussing how it might work if Mariner became chairman and CEO. Would I be willing to stay and work with Mariner, or would I choose to leave since this arrangement was clearly not what I had signed up for?

To his credit, Crosby told me privately that he would understand if I decided to pack it up and head back to Boston. Not being a quitter, I never strongly considered this. When I brought Michelle into the discussions, she didn't push in that direction either.

At a point when I did waver during the discussions over the weekend, it was Michelle who brought me back to center. We both felt that I had come to do a job and that the job was not yet finished. In fact, it had barely begun. Michelle reaffirmed her support and her willingness to move to Kansas City if that is what I wanted to do. It was important to me to have her support as we contemplated a final plan.

Mariner, a highly talented leader with strong instincts about business and people, held his father's long-standing commitment to conservative business and lending practices, but he was young and untested. Mariner had grown up with UMB, which was a strength and a weakness. He knew pretty much all there was to know about the company, its operations, and its culture. On the other hand, Mariner had only seen the company operated one way, with one leader, his dad, at the helm. That made for some blind spots when it came to alternative strategic and leadership approaches.

Complicating matters even more, Mariner had made it clear to his dad that under no circumstances would he move his family from Denver to

Kansas City. Not now, not ever. He went so far as to say that if this was a precondition of any expanded role, he would take a pass. I admired Mariner for his clarity and priorities in this regard.

However, this stipulation complicated things: Someone needed to be the face of the company to a constituency of more than 2.2 million people. Someone had to be UMB's Mr. Kansas City. I had not signed up for that role and lacked the relevant expertise and time in the community. Crosby III was supposed to be filling that role while I focused on running the company.

If Mariner, as CEO, remained in Denver, I would need to essentially perform both roles in Kansas City. That made the job significantly larger, more complex, but in many ways a lot more interesting than just being the "inside" person. It turned out that becoming Mr. Kansas City would be a game changer for me, something that completely expanded how I viewed my ability to make positive change in the world. It added a whole new dimension to my professional and personal mosaic. At the time, however, it felt overwhelming.

Before I agreed to the dual role, I needed to be sure that Michelle understood what the role would mean for her. Being the CEO of UMB Bank requires the spouse to also be immersed in the community.

In Boston, Michelle and I were an average couple with two kids making our way in the world. In this role in Kansas City, we would be thrust into the world of high society. There would be lots of community engagements, including black-tie fundraisers, dinners, participation on boards, and volunteer activity.

I was confident that Michelle was more than up to the challenge if she wanted to undertake it, but I did not want to force this on her. I remember her saying, "Calm down. We will figure this out together. Whatever happens, we will still have each other."

Michelle had the insight to recognize that the company institutionally possessed the platform we needed for the role and that we would receive ample support. We could count on the other senior leaders at the company, along with Crosby and other Kansas City-based members of the Kemper family, as we moved forward. Ultimately, we agreed to this new arrangement. I'm not sure either Michelle or I fully understood what we were getting ourselves into.

I felt strongly that I would need the right platform behind me to be successful in this new arrangement. This platform had to include the right role, responsibilities, and reporting relationships. It had to have real role clarity, the right titles, and the right decision-making authority. Mariner and I worked all that out in a seemingly never-ending but constructive conversation that Sunday.

Early the following week, the board elected Mariner chairman and CEO of UMB Financial Corporation. They elected me chairman and CEO of UMB Bank (the company's largest subsidiary), while also retaining my role and title as president and COO of UMB Financial Corporation. I had plenty of concerns about whether the plan was going to work, but it really was the best option available to us at the time.

When we announced the changes to the various constituencies, there was shock over the news that C-III was leaving under unclear circumstances but relief that there would be continuity with Mariner and me now leading the organization. We avoided a hostile takeover and/or a significant exodus of talent. Now it was up to Mariner and me to prove that the confidence of the board was well placed. While there were the inevitable bumps along the way, this arrangement worked well over the next twelve years.

Mariner and I got through the difficult first days, weeks, and months with a pledge to be transparent and to trust each other. We made a commitment to never let the other be surprised and to collaborate on key decisions. We checked our egos at the door and consistently did what was right for the company.

My early years at UMB were quite successful and rewarding. Mariner and I made numerous strategic, personnel, and cultural changes that began to alter the complexion of the company, not only in the eyes of the street and the community, but in the eyes of our associates, who in many ways were our most important constituency.

Mariner and I were hitting our stride as partners and collaborators, and we became close friends. We knew our respective lanes, with Mariner taking care of family business and focusing principally on commercial lending and the core banking side of the business. Mariner liked to say that he had been a banker since he was very young; his father always talked about the bank at the dinner table. Banking ran deep in the family and was in Mariner's blood.

I, on the other hand, focused on improving the core infrastructure of the company, building our money management and wealth management businesses, launching a health care services platform, growing our mutual fund service business, and building a comprehensive system of accountability measurements.

At the same time, I was making progress building a personal brand in the Kansas City community. This was a whole new experience for me. Being thrust into the external spotlight as a community leader and as the senior sales executive in the Kansas City market allowed me to grow, gain confidence, and make a difference. The experience redefined my understanding of an executive leader's opportunity and responsibility to make a positive impact in the world. More about this in Chapter 6. For now, it's enough to say that my mosaic was forever changed.

In any organization, leadership and culture starts at the top. UMB had the good fortune of having the same family at the helm for almost one hundred years. This stability was a real strength of the organization. UMB had a longstanding sense of purpose, an established set of core values, and a strong sense of the "right way," and the "UMB way" of doing things.

The company was well known for taking great care of its largest clients in a highly personalized manner. Our competitors knew that it was difficult to take good business away from UMB.

The company was also a leader in the broader Kansas City community. The family and the company had made tremendous contributions to the life of Kansas City since the company's founding.

The company's local brand, however, was more of a mixed bag. On one hand, business owners took comfort in our relationship-oriented approach and the care with which each relationship was handled. On the other hand, many felt that the company was far too risk-averse, which inhibited the growth of the company and the community. Banks are the lifeblood of any community. When they don't make credit available, the wheels of the local economy grind more slowly.

There was a saying in town that you could only get a loan from UMB if you had an equal amount of cash on deposit as collateral for the loan. This would all but ensure that the company had a minimal risk of loss. While this was not true, the impression was damaging.

Our competitors loved to use that line as a sales tactic against us saying, "Why even try to get a loan at UMB? Come do business with us where we actually make loans."

As a result, many business owners would not even consider doing business with UMB. We were allowing our competitors to define who we were rather than proactively defining who we were and communicating that to the community at large. We gave our competitors a potent competitive weapon to utilize against us. Crosby would often say that we didn't want all the business in town. We just wanted all the *best* business in town. This meant we only wanted the most creditworthy borrowers.

Conservatism ran deep in the company, not only in credit policy, but also in human resource policies. In addition, authoritative and sometimes rude leadership behavior often occurred without obvious consequences. Stories circulated of individuals being asked to leave the credit committee when a risky credit was presented or were verbally reprimanded in public when a loss occurred. Mariner and I knew the company needed to be modernized, and we set out to do it.

During my first year at the company, as I spent time in the community, a disturbing pattern emerged. I met dozens of individuals who had worked at UMB at some point in the past. People come and go from companies for different reasons, but I kept hearing the same troubling reason again and again: The UMB culture was not positive, uplifting, or associate-centered. Rather than appealing to emerging professionals and leaders, the culture was viewed as old-fashioned, stale, and out of date. It was a place to be *from*, not to be *at*.

UMB had inadvertently become the training ground for the other banks and financial institutions in the region. I needed to know more about why we were losing our valuable talent to the competition, and I needed to know fast. Then we needed to do something about it, pronto. Mariner and I agreed to make this one of our top goals and make UMB a destination for talent rather than a provider of talent to other companies. We knew a large part of our ultimate success would be tied to sourcing, hiring, developing, and retaining the finest talent. We needed to create an employer brand as strong as our customer brand.

It takes great people, led and motivated the right way, to achieve great things. To repeat one of my most strongly held beliefs, if you take care of your associates, they will take care of your customers, and the rest will take care of itself. Having seen this principle in action in my own young career at Cinema 140, it has been one of the hallmarks of my leadership style. This approach, when properly activated, has proven to be true everywhere I have gone throughout my career.

Leaders talk endlessly about the client experience, but many do not understand the inextricable connection between the associate experience and the client experience. It is not possible to have an extraordinary client experience without an extraordinary associate experience.

I started asking questions of current associates, former associates, and the community at large about what it was like to be a UMB associate. Internally, we held dozens of focus groups, conducted associate surveys, and held one-on-one meetings in pursuit of actionable answers. What I heard was alarming: Our talent told us they were dissatisfied and disenchanted with the company for several reasons. The leadership style was outdated, not in keeping with what associates expected in a contemporary employee/employer relationship. For example, the practice of calling people out in front of others and other unacceptable old-school behaviors continued. Advancement opportunities were often more based on who you knew versus how you performed. Conservative risk polices significantly inhibited growth, limiting opportunities for career growth and increased compensation.

Associates felt they were stuck rather than moving forward in their careers. The highest performing ones had no reason to stay with the company. Reward systems, including compensation programs and sales commissions, were significantly outdated. As a result, hard work and prudent risk-taking were often not properly rewarded. The company had no sales incentives, even for loans made within the conservative criteria of the organization. In terms of providing service, the company's technology and tools were past their sell-by date, inhibiting the ability to deliver excellent service.

Once Mariner and I had a sense of the issues we needed to resolve, we got right to work. A top order of business was to recruit a new leader of human resources (HR) who was significantly more contemporary in terms of thinking and practices to help us bridge the gaps we had uncovered.

I searched my personal archive and remembered Larry Smith, a colleague from Fidelity. Larry was an exceptional HR leader, someone who always had time for people and made those around him better. He understood the power of people who were motivated and properly rewarded. He also had firsthand knowledge of the destructive elements that can occur when the opposite is true. We were fortunate enough to recruit Larry to assist us with the cultural and leadership journey ahead. Larry helped us begin the process of changing policies and procedures to make UMB a more positive place for our associates.

It wasn't long before something even more important started to influence the culture as well. I am unsure if it was conscious on either of our parts, or just a function of our comfort with each other and the trust Mariner and I had built up between us. Whatever the reason, the organization began to see Mariner and me relaxed and having fun together. This was a stark difference from the stuffy corporate culture that had existed previously.

I remember being on stage with Mariner at various company functions and the two of us simply enjoying each other's company, teasing each other, and laughing. The way we worked together began to influence how others felt about the organization. The comradery and trust began to rub off on others. I felt that we were on our way.

While it was clear that we were making progress on the associate value proposition, I still felt that we needed to make a statement to the associates, our competitors, and the broader community about our commitment to durable change. A strong associate value proposition is akin to a strong customer value proposition. Without a strong customer value proposition, customers go elsewhere. Exactly the same phenomenon takes place with associates. Without a strong associate value proposition, associates seek out and find organizations that more closely resemble their view of the relationship they desire from an employer.

Developing Emerging Talent with Fences

Mariner and I fought the talent war on multiple levels. While we were building a top-notch leadership team, we were also identifying and taking smart risks on emerging leaders. For example, shortly after arriving at UMB, William Short, a management trainee, took the initiative to leave a white paper on my desk extolling the virtues of health savings accounts (HSAs). Intrigued, I set up a few minutes with William so he could further lay out the business case. He quickly impressed me as a sharp, thoughtful, high energy twenty-something with an air of self-confidence. This was just the kind of emerging leader we needed at UMB.

Health savings accounts were established when President George W. Bush signed the Medicare Prescription Drug, Improvement, and Modernization Act of 2003. An HSA can only be utilized as a complement to high-deductible health plans, which employers were just beginning to offer. HSAs function much like 401Ks, except they are utilized to save for and pay for costs related to health care versus retirement needs.

The essence of the business case William presented was that HSAs were about to explode as 401K plans had since their inception in 1978. The thesis was that employers would be interested in migrating to high-deductible health plans from the current plan design. This would lower plan costs for employers by shifting some of the burden onto individual participants.

For their part, employees would like the idea of making a lower premium payment as they could deposit the difference between the higher premium cost under a traditional plan, and the lower premium cost under a high-deductible plan into a tax deferred bank of brokerage Health Savings Account in which they could earn interest, or even invest in the stock market. I had seen the massive growth of the 401K marketplace over the prior two decades from my vantage point at Fidelity. I became convinced that UMB could replicate that success in the HSA space. The question was how to develop the capability and effectively leverage this huge potential opportunity.

Even though William had come up with the idea, I was not about to hand him total responsibility for its execution. He was a young leader who had never had responsibility for what was likely to be a large, high-profile, costly, and risky undertaking. I decided to allow William to play a significant role in the product's development but only with an appropriate fence (boundaries and support of a seasoned leader) around him. Having William lead this project would accelerate his growth and development, but I did not want him to fail.

I called on Dennis Triplett to take William under his wing. Dennis was a long-time UMB veteran who had built the bank's deposit and consumer banking systems over many years. Dennis had significant cross-company credibility and was a strong leader.

I asked Dennis to allow William to run as far and fast as he could under his watchful oversight. Additionally, we established measurable milestones and goals, spending limits, technology resourcing budgets, weekly and monthly leadership updates, and other ways to monitor progress and quickly resolve issues as they arose.

The process was not all roses. There were many incidents throughout the journey where the limits of the fences were tested. There were issues with overspending, internal squabbles, and delays in delivery. At more than one point, I gave serious consideration to scuttling the program. It was consuming our limited resources and becoming a distraction to our core commercial and consumer banking business. However, we were determined to make it work.

Throughout the program, I adjusted the contours of the fences as I gained confidence in William, Dennis, and the team. These resets were deliberate on my part, and they allowed the team the freedom and accountability they needed to pursue the plan. Today, UMB ranks as one of the top five providers of HSA account services in what has become a $100 billion industry. It all started by taking a risk on an emerging leader and building a fence around him. I learned my lesson from the way Fred Knapp handled another young, budding leader early in his career.

Since my earliest days with the company, I had heard of Bill Greiner, the former chief investment officer for UMB bank. Bill had been well liked and had an excellent reputation as an investment professional. Unfortunately, Bill was one of the executives who had resigned after numerous conflicts with previous bank leadership. He did not want to work in a contemptuous environment.

Crosby Jr. and Mariner thought highly of Bill and acknowledged that it was unfortunate that he had left the company. Although both also interpreted his departure as disloyal, they agreed to welcome Bill Greiner back if we could attract him. I went to work.

When Bill agreed to have dinner with me, I saw, as others did, a smart, thoughtful, sincere, and insightful investment professional full of integrity. When I asked why he left UMB, Bill would only say that the culture was not agreeable to him. People were treated in ways he could not tolerate.

When I asked if he'd be willing to consider coming back, Bill said, "I have been watching what you and Mariner are doing at the company. It is impressive. The people I talk to speak of a new, more positive, open, and transparent culture. I hear it's a fun place to be, a company on the move again."

I was elated, knowing that if we could attract Bill back to the company, it would send a huge message, especially internally, that the culture was changing for the better. Mariner and I had addressed the leadership behavior, and destructive conflict would no longer be tolerated. The message was likely to spread to the broader business community that things were changing at UMB for the better.

Within a few weeks we were able to announce Bill's return as chief investment officer to extremely favorable internal and external reviews. While Bill's return was an important milestone in the evolution of the company and its culture, an even more significant hire would soon rock the Midwest banking community.

One day, a couple of years into my tenure, Crosby Jr. suggested that I have a chat with Clyde Wendel, president, Kansas City Region and regional executive for Bank of America Private Bank. Having chatted with Clyde at a recent function, Crosby intuited that Clyde might be ready for a change. Initially I was doubtful. After all, Clyde had been at Bank of America and its predecessors for decades and was well regarded locally and nationally. Clyde was one of Kansas City's finest community leaders. Still, I set up a dinner with Clyde to see what I could uncover.

My expectations for the meeting were quite low. I figured we would get to know each other a little bit, talk about business, have a nice dinner, and then go our separate ways. I was wrong. About halfway through dinner, it became apparent that Crosby's intuition was correct. Clyde was unhappy at Bank of America. Under the right circumstances, he might consider a move to UMB. But first, he had some hard questions for me.

He noted that it seemed from the outside that Mariner and I were changing the culture in a positive way. Clyde had also seen UMB become more competitive in making loans over the past few years. He wanted to know if these changes were real and sustainable or just window dressing. He wanted to know if Mariner and I had Crosby's and the board's support for our actions. He also wanted to know if he would have the authority to make the decisions he thought needed to be made within his domain, including associate-related decisions.

I assured Clyde that the changes he and others were seeing were indeed real; that Mariner, Crosby, and the board were 100 percent committed to new culture; and that we would empower him to make whatever changes he thought necessary to advance the parts of the organization entrusted to him. Once Clyde was comfortable with my assurances, we discussed the rough contours of what a role might look like. We both left intrigued, but there was still more work to do before reaching an agreement.

The next morning, I reviewed the details of the meeting with Mariner. We decided that we needed to have Clyde—no matter the cost. This hire would make a huge statement about the positive changes in our culture and prospects for UMB's future to the community, our associates, and our competitors. Someone of Clyde Wendel's caliber would not switch companies lightly.

On June 9, 2006, we issued a press release announcing that Clyde would be joining UMB as president of UMB's asset management and managing director of UMB Private Banking. He would be nominated to serve as vice chairman of UMB Bank, National Association, and would be a member of the company's Management Committee.

The story made front-page news in the *Kansas City Star* that day. It is not customary for a business story, especially one about the hiring of an executive, to be above the fold on the front page of the paper, but there it was. We had pulled off a real coup, and the community and our competitors took notice. UMB was back in a big way.

Over the next few years, as our performance improved and the culture was modernized, more and more executives wanted to be part of the team. One of the things I am most proud of from my twelve years at UMB is the updating of the company's culture and the high-quality leadership team we assembled. We were now a destination employer. A place to be at, not a place to be from. We had set out to attract and retain the best and we were succeeding.

As the culture improved, new talent provided enhanced energy, and outdated human resources policies and procedures were updated, the organization developed a bit of a swagger. In former times, some of our associates would put their heads down when asked where they worked. Now, they puffed out their chests and proudly said that they worked for UMB.

Within a few years, our associate engagement scores had reached best-in-class levels, specifically against banks and other financial companies. It was a marked contrast from where we started. At UMB we were truly beginning to live the associate-centered part of our commitment.

About this time, we received a testament to our progress from an unexpected source. Several UMB associates from across the hierarchy stopped Michelle on the streets of Kansas City to express their appreciation for the positive culture and opportunities for growth and advancement we had created. Michelle took great satisfaction in these encounters, recognizing afresh that creating workplaces where individuals can flourish positively affects families.

The second part of the equation in remaking the company was elevating the customer experience. In that regard, we were on a journey to rethink every part of the company and our approach to deliver a superior client experience. The effort started with a new vision which was "to deliver the *unparalleled* customer experience."

To state this as an absolute was bold and brash. The Walt Disney Company had pioneered the concept of customer experience at its theme parks by incorporating the time spent waiting in line into the experience of the ride. In the 1990s, Fidelity, under Ned Johnson's leadership, had been among the first companies to recognize that client service expectations were rapidly rising as new technologies went mainstream.

Ned Johnson was passionate about the customer experience. During my tenure with Fidelity, I had been part of the team responsible to move the company from customer service to customer experience. By now, Disney, Ritz Carlton, Starbucks, and others had built their entire businesses around a strong customer experience.

At first, I was quite concerned about this vision statement. Could we really redefine an unparalleled customer experience? Did we have the capabilities, the willpower, and the resources to deliver? How were we going to prove that our experience was *unparalleled*?

After reviewing the definition in the dictionary, I became even more concerned. According to Merriam-Webster, unparalleled means "having no equal or match." That is a tall order. Despite my concerns, this is what the team agreed to set out to do.

The experience was one of several that taught me about the power of painting a powerful, positive, aspirational view of the future. I had seen Ned Johnson do this at Fidelity, and now Mariner and I were doing it at UMB. We knew we were setting a stretch goal for ourselves, something we might not actually attain in a practical sense. Still, the fact that we had created a BHAG (a big hairy audacious goal) motivated the team.

We followed our new vison with a strong brand promise. A brand promise is a value or experience that a company's customers can expect to receive every single time they interact with the company. The more a company can deliver on that promise, the stronger the brand value is in the minds of customers and employees.

We launched our brand promise as "Count on More." This statement was a promise to our clients and a set of expectations for our associates. If we were going to promise more in every interaction, our associates had to be the mechanism by which we delivered it. We began to run campaigns that emphasized the word *more*: More service. More caring. More advocacy. More community.

We launched a scholarship program for associates and their families called the UMB Count on More Scholarship Program, and we named a lounge in the downtown Kansas City Sprint Center Arena the UMB Count on More Lounge. This became a place where we could entertain clients and exceed their expectations when treating them to a sporting event or live entertainment. We were so pleased with the motivational power of these three words that in October 2008 we trademarked the phrase.

While we were working on a refreshed brand for UMB, I was aware that I had a brand of my own as a leader, although I wouldn't have used that terminology at the time. The days of LinkedIn and executive brand specialists were still in the future. At the time, leaders simply needed to be aware of their image.

I intentionally projected the image of a strong, confident, transparent, and decisive leader. I wanted to be known for my integrity, collaboration, and commitment to facts and people. I was careful never to project myself as weak in any way.

Since my Little League days, I was insecure and distanced myself from anything that hinted at vulnerability. I was aware that I didn't have a fancy pedigree and hadn't attended an Ivy League school. More than anything else, I was acutely aware that I had a secret ailment, my CMT.

I had learned from my dad to make the most of what life had given me, and I was proud of who I was and what I had accomplished. Still, I probably worked harder than was healthy for me because I felt that I always had to prove myself. The two things I feared most were being limited in opportunities because of my CMT and being the object of anyone's pity.

Given this context, it was a shock to me when my niece, Amy, then around age twelve, decided to go 100 percent public with her CMT. She became a spokesperson for the Charcot-Marie-Tooth Association (CMTA), an organization dedicated to providing support and resources on behalf of those suffering from CMT. Amy, who has a beautiful voice, even sang for CMTA.

I could appreciate and was proud of Amy's choice to work for an important personal cause. I was also proud of Amy's accomplishments as a singer. I arranged for her to sing the National Anthem at a Kansas City Royals baseball game and brought the family out to share the moment. I couldn't have been more impressed by this young woman.

Still, I didn't for a minute consider going public with my own CMT. Rather than stand alongside Amy publicly, I distanced myself. I was adamant about not setting myself up to be limited or pitied.

I remember a day when Amy's mom—my sister-in-law Cathy—challenged me to get more involved, saying, "You have the ability to help, Peter, and you are not doing it. Why won't you get involved?"

I responded, "My health is my issue. It is a private matter. The way I deal with it is my business. I'm not getting involved." I donated money here and there, but I refused to get deeply involved. I was determined not to be a public face for CMT.

Around that time, I met and became friendly with Patrick Livney, who was then the CEO of CMTA. I even attended a CMTA board meeting. Pat, who also has CMT, kept admonishing me, "Peter, you've got to get involved. You've got to do more. You can't just give money. We need you on the board. We need you be a face for this."

I pushed back, "I'm not doing it. I'll give you all the money I can. In terms of being a face, I'm just not going to do it."

Taking stock from my vantage point today, my stance was misguided and selfish. My stubborn pride ruled the day. Even in the face of Amy,

Lynne, and Sarah's struggles with symptoms, I didn't change my view. I was overly concerned with my personal brand and blinded to the power I had to help others. I am saddened by the opportunities I wasted at that time.

When you seek to build unique customer experiences, you quickly recognize that your traditional competitors—in our case, other banks or financial services companies—are not your only competition. When you choose to compete on customer experience, every other business is your competitor. This sets an incredibly high bar. Count on more in *every* experience? While challenging, this is the right bar for any company or organization that aspires to be top-of-mind for its clients and prospects.

We were embracing that high bar. Over time, we needed a way to empirically demonstrate this commitment to ourselves, our shareholders, and our associates. As I sat in my office looking over various reports one day, a realization struck me. We needed to answer the question: What is the correlation between associate engagement, client satisfaction, and operating results? How tight is this correlation? Could we demonstrate that creating a unique set of associate experiences was the primary driver in delivering superior operating results? I had to find out.

Mariner and I gave the HR and finance teams the challenge to see if we could make this claim. They came back to us shortly thereafter and reported that the research showed a tight correlation between these three strategic variables. Now we had evidence that focusing on the associate experience was not only the right thing to do for the associates—it was the right thing to do for the firm, its clients, and its shareholders.

In 2008, we began to show a chart in our annual report that demonstrated the link between associate engagement and our operating results. In 2004, the year that Mariner and I took over, the company had an associate engagement score of 57 percent and earnings of $42.8 million. Here are the results from 2004 through 2011.

Year	Associate Engagement	Customer Sat.	Earnings (in millions)
2004	57%	N/A	$42.8
2005	62%	N/A	$56.3
2006	69%	N/A	$59.8
2007	73%	N/A	$74.2
2008	82%	65%	$98.1
2009	84%	56%	$89.5
2010	82%	63%	$91.0
2011	84%	67%	$106.5

In the 2009 UMB Financial Corporation Annual Report, I wrote these words to shareholders:

> At UMB, our associates are our most important assets. Without the best people and the best people practices, we can't meet our customers' needs. Creating a performance culture means we uphold the highest standards, and we demand the best from our products, our services, and ourselves.

As I worked with Mariner, I continued to have an excellent relationship with his father, Crosby Jr. I remember him beaming with pride as he shared stories about the positive things his friends were saying to him about the changes they, as clients or board members, were experiencing at UMB. I took pride in the fact that Crosby was proud of the company that he had stewarded for so long. I wanted nothing more than to make him proud of the institution into which he had poured his life.

After Crosby's death on January 2, 2014, however, a process of change began to unfold. Mariner's behavior toward me slowly shifted. At the age of thirty-nine, Mariner was now effectively the family patriarch, leading the family's most significant asset, UMB Financial Corporation. He faced the pressures associated with that role, along with the ones associated with the role of leading the family's charitable foundations and other business affairs. I suspect there were many voices inside and outside the company, along with some family voices, that contributed to his changing approach.

At first, the changes were subtle; I was no longer invited to certain meetings and events. Then came a series of structural changes. Some departments that had been reporting to me shifted to either Mariner or our CFO, Mike Hagedorn. Because of my trust in Mariner, and the fact that I knew he needed to adjust in the face of his father's passing, I did not make much of the changes. My objective was not to add to the burden he was already carrying. Despite our close relationship, this was business, and Mariner was doing what he deemed was right for the organization.

As 2014 went along, Mariner made more organizational changes, resulting in even more responsibility being split between Mariner, Mike, and me. I tried to understand the reasoning behind some of the changes. Still, for the first time in our ten-plus-year relationship, distance began to stand between the two of us.

Mariner never lost his collaborative nature, but he seemed to think that his new circumstances required deeper involvement in the inner workings of the organization. At this juncture, the company was performing extremely well, so I didn't believe the shifts were about any performance concerns, either mine or the company's. If Mariner had concerns about my performance, he never expressed them to me. My reviews were stellar, and my annual bonuses and share awards were consistently at or above the top end of the range.

As you might expect, there were always complex and difficult business issues to work through. For example, we needed an enhanced strategy to accelerate the growth of Scout Investments. Despite all our success building that part of the organization, there were constant pressures from larger, more well-heeled competitors with bigger brands, better distribution, and sometimes even better performance. There were pressures to accelerate the growth of our commercial lending business while preserving the strong credit quality that was our hallmark.

These kinds of business issues were not new. In the past, we had worked through them as a team. At this time, however, Mariner seemed less inclined to accept some of my views than he had been. He was in charge, and it seemed more and more as if he needed everyone to know it. I was never sure how much of this was Mariner's choice versus pressure from others. In any case, things were changing, and in terms of my role at the company, not for the better.

Three Zones of Control

I have observed over time that a person operates in three mutually exclusive but connected zones in business and personal life. The three zones are control, influence, and neither control nor influence. I call the latter the punt zone. The best leaders understand which zone they are operating in during any given situation. They work to exploit that zone to their advantage.

Events you completely control include the time you get up in the morning, your attitude on any given day or situation, and the level of effort you put into your work. In such cases, there are no excuses for nonperformance. You own it. Make it yours and make it good. I estimate that I spend about 25 percent of my time in this zone, doing things that I completely control.

There are always events and situations you do not or cannot control. Consider, for example, most business meetings. Assuming there is no sole decision maker, individuals with different perspectives and agendas try to influence the meeting outcome, often in ways most advantageous to themselves. Or consider being in Congress where 435 House members and one hundred Senators try to influence each other in search of common ground. The best thing you can do in these instances is to attempt to influence the outcome. While operating in this zone can be extremely frustrating, it is where leaders spend most of their time. I estimate that I spend 50 to 60 percent of my time in this zone.

The way to be most effective in the second zone is to present strong facts and data, along with sound, logical arguments, and common sense and reason. It can also be helpful to use storytelling to personalize a case. The alternative is to present your arguments without hard facts and with emotion to evoke a response. Without facts that can be backed up, all you have is an emotional response. I am not suggesting that you should not display emotion as you seek to persuade, just that facts and data are the foundation upon which you can utilize emotion to make your point.

It's critically important to recognize when you are in the third zone, where you have neither control nor influence over the decision or outcome. The weather provides a good example. None of us has any control over the weather, yet we spend endless amounts of time thinking and worrying about it. The same is often true in business situations, especially in a private company where the outcomes can be determined by a single individual or a small ownership group. When you can't control or influence a situation, you must adjust. This is where I found myself with Mariner following his father's death.

The zone in which you have neither control nor influence can be extremely destructive. If you spend too much time in this zone, you waste precious time and effort that should be focused on the things you can control or at least influence. If you want to be an effective leader, get out of this zone as quickly as you can and accept reality. It's time to punt the ball and move on.

Following the fall 2014 board meeting, which was held in Denver that quarter rather than Kansas City, Mariner indicated to me that he once again wanted to reorganize the company and further realign the scope of my responsibilities. He claimed these changes were about achieving greater focus, but it felt like another opportunity to shrink my portfolio of responsibilities.

Some voices in the organization were advocating for a return to the way things had been before Mariner and I began working together as a team. Maybe this was because of their inability to embrace change or because they had lost influence in the new environment. I suspect that these voices may have contributed to the new relationship challenges between Mariner and me. We were at a critical tipping point. For the first time in a long time, I began to think seriously about whether I wanted to be part of the UMB organization. Although Mariner claimed that he wanted me to stay, and I wanted to believe him, his actions seemed to indicate otherwise.

I flew home from Denver following the board meeting, knowing that I was scheduled to attend a Kansas City Royals game that evening to entertain associates and bank clients. I had hosted these sorts of client events scores of times in the past, but none when I was seriously thinking about my future at the company. I considered not going to the game, but my sense of responsibility pushed me forward. I put on a brave face and went to the game. I was able to be gracious to my guests at the game and even enjoy some of the conversations. The decision before me, however, was nagging in the background. I needed to update Michelle and have a conversation with her about what to do.

Michelle and I spent much of the weekend wrestling with the choices before us. We realized that it was time for me to leave UMB, but that didn't make acting on that realization easy. I was proud of the significant contribution I had made in my years at the company. I had made a difference in the life of Kansas City and the broader region, and I was proud of that too. Sometimes, however, a good run comes to an end, and it is time to move on. This was one of those times.

Upon deeper reflection, I concluded that I had stayed too long in the first place. I had become comfortable and complacent. I had a good thing going. But, somewhere along the way, I stopped learning and growing. I came to realize that I had been going through the motions. While I had the major challenges of my role, I was no longer being stretched the way I wanted and needed to be.

Also, after almost twelve years at UMB, I had reached a point of disequilibrium with Mariner and the company. I could not see how we could work together effectively any longer. Mariner was in a new place, with different needs. Our strong historic working relationship and friendship could no longer carry the day.

The announcement of my departure from UMB was met with shock across the company, the investor community, and the broader Kansas City business and philanthropic community. There had been no obvious warning. Even some of the board members were surprised that I was leaving.

In the days following the announcement, I received hundreds of cards, emails, and other acknowledgments from associates, clients, board members, and community leaders. It felt great to know that my accomplishments had been noticed and appreciated. I had loved and extended my best self to the organization, the company, and the community. Michelle had done the same. Although we had sacrificed much, the payback in terms of friendships and enduring contributions was well worth the effort.

Over the next few weeks, I started to look for my next opportunity. I believe you need to work as hard at finding the right job as working at that job. I started contacting my deep network of business and recruiting contacts to see what roles might be available. Within a few weeks, I was fortunate to have three bona fide offers. One was to become CEO of a St. Louis-based bank; another was to become a C-suite leader at a Kansas City-based national telecommunications company; and a third was to become president of a large national St. Louis-based broker-dealer/online trading firm.

I remember the angst as Michelle and I sorted through three extremely compelling offers. I had hammered out the details of all three deals, had met with board members from two of the three, and was getting pressure from all sides to decide. As I always do when I have a difficult decision to make, I built a matrix of the costs, benefits, and challenges associated with each opportunity.

In the end, I chose to return to my roots in the brokerage and wealth management business by accepting the offer to become president of Scottrade Financial Services in St. Louis. This meant another move, this time to the eastern side of Missouri. I chose the Scottrade opportunity for several important reasons that I'll relate in an upcoming chapter.

For now, I want to take stock of the time I spent representing UMB as a community leader in Kansas City. That role had a powerful impact on my mosaic and was a critical factor in my later choice to participate in Harvard's ALI program.

Chapter 6

Discovering a New World of Leadership Possibilities:
Kansas City

The Kansas City community and region is firmly rooted in its proud past while looking with confidence to an even brighter future. Given its central geographic location, Kansas City is sometimes known as the heart of America. Even its airport, Mid-Continent International Airport (now Kansas City International Airport), recognized this fact. With two cities claiming the same name—Kansas City, Missouri, and Kansas City, Kansas—this Midwest community also confuses much of America.

The broader community is divided by state lines, the Missouri River, and many different counties, which can make cohesive governance challenging. It is a community that proudly looks west, while St. Louis, on Missouri's eastern side, looks east. It is said that Missouri is as far east as the west goes. As far west as the east goes. As far north as the south goes. And as far south as the north goes, which makes for a very interesting state: almost a geographical melting pot.

Kansas City was America's first western city. In 1804, Lewis and Clark spent time at the confluence of the Missouri and Kaw Rivers exploring the area. In 1860, the Pony Express, the first fast mail line across the North American continent, started in St. Joseph, Missouri, and ended in Sacramento, California. And the Santa Fe, Oregon, and California trails all either passed through or emanated from Kansas City.

Long before Dallas and Phoenix became what they are today, Kansas City was the largest and strongest western-facing city in America. This was so significant that in 1963 Lamar Hunt, owner of the then Dallas Texans, selected Kansas City as the place to relocate his football franchise, counting on the strength of the city and its anticipated future growth. Hunt would rename the team the Kansas City Chiefs in recognition of H. Roe Bartle, Kansas City's mayor at the time, who was the "chief" of the fictional Boy Scouts Tribe of Mic-O-Say.

In recognition of Kansas City's dramatic growth in the early part of the twentieth century, the Federal Reserve created a new Federal Reserve Bank of Kansas City in 1914, headquartered in the fast-growing community and making Missouri the only state with two Reserve Banks (one in St. Louis (looking east), and the other in Kansas City (looking west).

Unlike other communities that can be parochial or even hostile to newcomers, Kansas City's established business and civic leaders welcome newcomers with open arms. Because of the strength of UMB's business and civic platform, Michelle and I were invited to participate in practically every facet of the community's business and civic life. At first, Michelle and I were intimidated by the strength, depth, and legacy of the community leaders. We often asked ourselves what we could offer this community to which we had just relocated.

I quickly learned that community engagement is a full-contact sport. Both of us would need to be all in. Michelle would need to support my community pursuits on behalf of UMB, and she would need to be her own person, with her own interests and pursuits. Thankfully, Michelle was comfortable in this position and more than willing to get fully engaged in our new community. She chose to consult with the Greater Kansas City Community Foundation, one of the largest community foundations in the US, with over $5.4 billion in assets as of December 2021. She also joined the boards of numerous nonprofit organizations.

We came to understand that Kansas City was home to several families that had built successful companies there and chosen to give back to their hometown community. The companies included Hallmark Cards, Sprint, Cerner (now Oracle Cerner), H&R Block, Burns & McDonnell, Commerce Bank, UMB Bank, American Multimedia Cinemas (AMC), Black & Veatch, JE Dunn Construction, Kansas City Southern Railway, American Century Investments, DST Systems, Garmin, Marion Laboratories, and others. Additionally, Kansas City is home to the Ewing Marion Kauffman Foundation, a global foundation dedicated to "build and support programs that improve education, boost entrepreneurship, and help our hometown of Kansas City thrive." The foundation would play a vital role in supporting my efforts to build a more entrepreneurial Kansas City.

You'll recall that I did not go to Kansas City expecting to be a community leader. Things had been working beautifully with my "inside role" until Crosby III suddenly resigned from his position as CEO at UMB. When Mariner chose not to relocate from Denver to Kansas City, I needed to be the primary public face of UMB. I was challenged to quickly develop new skills, abilities, and relationships and figure out how to balance my time between my inside and outside activities. So much for being the invisible inside person.

I remember sitting with Crosby Jr. shortly after Mariner and I took responsibility for UMB to strategize about my role in the Kansas City community. He recommended a few organizations for me to get involved with right away. These were the Kansas City Symphony, the Greater Kansas City Chamber of Commerce, Park University, and the United Way of Greater Kansas City. In short order, I was elected to the boards of these respective organizations.

From the early days of my career, I understood the critical importance of building enduring relationships. After all, I wouldn't even be in my position at UMB were it not for my long-term relationship with the Kemper family.

I knew that mutually supportive relationships were essential in getting things done in a community or an organization. When asking for financial support or other forms of resources, success is based one-third on what the ask is *for*, and two-thirds on *who* is doing the asking. Developing strong, trusting community relationships would be necessary for success in my community work. Serving on these boards was a good way to begin reaching out and building those relationships.

I was particularly pleased to join the board of the United Way of Greater Kansas City. Since my early days at Fidelity when I was a reluctant team captain, I have been a champion of the United Way. The social safety net the United Way provides is essential in every community across America. One of the challenge phrases I like to use is, "But for . . ."

In this instance, *but for* the United Way, who would take care of those most in need? *But for* the United Way, how would those who need support navigate the myriad of social support programs? *But for* the United Way, how would social impact organizations collaborate across multiple domains?

One morning in early 2007, I had breakfast with Tom Dugard, president of the United Way of Greater Kansas City. Tom asked me to chair the annual Tocqueville Society fundraising event, a program to enroll United Way donors who pledge at least $10,000 annually.

I quickly told Tom that I had not been in the community long enough; I did not have the deep personal connections and relationships necessary for such an important task. He assured me that I had already earned credibility across the community and that he and his organization would support my efforts. At that point, I wasn't sure if he meant that I had the personal credibility or that the UMB platform gave me the institutional credibility to make these asks. Maybe it was both. I knew that Tom was selling that day, hoping I would buy. I did not buy on that day, but eventually I did.

One of the reasons I said yes was because I finally recognized the opportunity this role presented for me. The role would enable me to build my relationship muscle while raising much needed funds for the underserved in my community. Rather than perceive my being thrust into a public role before I had community relationships established as a disadvantage, I shifted my attitude. This role presented a golden opportunity to build relationships and accelerate my growth.

The Power of Enduring Relationships in All Aspects of Life

In life, business, and community work, enduring relationships—ones built on trust and ongoing mutual benefit—are essential. Successful leaders and individuals invest time and energy in building these relationships inside and outside their organizations and families.

Consider a personal relationship in which one spouse continually attempts to engage with the other, but to no avail, or the friend who is always the one reaching out to set up time to get together. A sense of disequilibrium starts to set in, and the relationship breaks apart. The same dynamic exists in a business relationship. If the parties cannot achieve ongoing equilibrium—the sense that each party is equally giving and receiving—a parting of the ways is the most likely outcome. This sense of disequilibrium is the primary reason why most individuals leave companies.

Working alongside others on projects to better the Kansas City community allowed me to connect with others and establish relationships characterized by a commitment that both parties equally give and take. When people roll up their sleeves in pursuit of a shared aspirational challenge, relationship barriers tend to break down.

Of course, not all relationships are enduring. Others are transactional, characterized by short-term or momentary benefits to the individuals or groups. Transactional relationships are exchanges in which "you do something for me, and I do something for you." There is no commitment beyond the current transaction.

Transactional relationships are a factor in all our lives. We all, for example, have transactional relationships with the cashier in the grocery store. We have them on short-term project teams and in many other business relationships. Transactional relationships can last for moments or years. They are not inherently bad; they are just transitory.

A critical characteristic of an enduring relationship is equilibrium. This is when each party is committed to ongoing mutual benefit. Both parties share resources and support on an ongoing basis, beyond any

> specific tasks. When a task or project is completed, both parties make the effort to stay connected, informed, and in support of the other's goals. There are no shortcuts when it comes to building these relationships.
>
> If you aspire to a meaningful life that accomplishes great things, you need to develop a broad network of mutually beneficial relationships. Personally and professionally, I owe a great deal to the people in my network. For example, I continue to enjoy and benefits from my relationship with Roger Lockwood, my first CEO, friend, and lifelong mentor. My relationships with members of the Kemper family—while working at Fidelity—led Crosby Jr. to reach out when they needed a new leader. I'll never know exactly what influences led to me getting the offer at TD Ameritrade later in my career, but David Kimm, a respected Fidelity colleague, was by then TD Ameritrade's chief risk officer and a direct report to TD Ameritrade CEO Tim Hockey. My continued friendship with Rodger Riney, Scottrade's founder and CEO, is another example.
>
> The relationships Michelle and I built in the Kansas City community and in the other communities we lived in have enriched our lives in countless ways. For example, although we haven't lived in Kansas City for years, those relationships continue to support my goals even in my third chapter of life. I'll tell that story in a later chapter.

Starting in 2009, the Kansas City Chamber launched a groundbreaking effort to create what amounted to a cohesive strategic plan for the region. This was the brainchild of the chamber's chair Anne St. Peter, CEO of Global Prairie. The chamber canvassed the business, political, and civic communities, along with residents of both sides of the state line, to identify the most meaningful opportunities to promote economic growth and improve the quality of life for all residents. In all, 182 proposals were put forth for consideration. Following extensive community-wide analysis, discussion, and debate, the chamber settled on five big ideas, the "Big 5:"

1. **Host the World Symposium on Animal Health.** Why not? After all, over 32 percent of the $19 billion global animal health market is accounted for by companies that stretch from Manhattan, Kansas, to Columbia, Missouri, with Kansas City right at the center.

2. **Revitalize Kansas City's urban core.** Like many large American cities, Kansas City's urban core had gone through an extended period of underinvestment. New investment would be needed to reconnect and revitalize what were formerly vital parts of the community.

3. **Build a new downtown conservatory for the University of Missouri-Kansas City (UMKC), the state university designated for the visual and performing arts.** The current facilities were inferior. The strategy was to move the conservatory downtown to provide new facilities, create energy, and support the renaissance that was underway downtown.

4. **Become a national leader in life sciences** with the goal being to "grow Kansas City's medical research from discovery to cure" and become a nationally recognized leader in translational research.

5. **Make Kansas City America's most entrepreneurial city.** This goal was to leverage the community's strong history of entrepreneurship and innovation, with the assistance of the Ewing Marion Kauffman Foundation, the UMKC Henry W. Bloch School of Management, local business leaders, and entrepreneurs to create a comprehensive ecosystem for the region's entrepreneurs.

These were big, bold, and audacious goals, the kind that sometimes fail to get real traction and end up as shelfware. That would not be the case in this instance.

In 2010, I was elected chair of the chamber board and continued the work on the Big 5 that my friend Anne had started. Meanwhile, an exciting new challenge emerged.

I honestly can't remember who whispered it to me first, but as soon as I heard the idea to relocate the headquarters of the Greater Kansas City Chamber of Commerce upon the expiration of its current lease from downtown Kansas City, Missouri, to historic Union Station in Midtown, I was sold. To me, it just made sense for the regional chamber to lead the effort to ensure the long-term viability of this historic station.

In 1996, in a rare display of regional cooperation, the residents on both sides of the Missouri and Kansas state line had voted to impose a tax on themselves to restore and revitalize the beautiful landmark. In 1999, the station reopened to the public as an event space with retail and a science museum. Things hadn't gone entirely as planned, and a decade later, the beautifully restored station was struggling to make ends meet. Something had to be done. We could not let this community treasure fall into disrepair again.

I was warned that there would be dissenting views about relocating the chamber and its sister organization, the Kansas City Area Development Council, to Union Station along with other civic groups. After all, the building was old and would need to be reconfigured to create efficient and modern office space. This created some unknowns, including the total time and cost of the retrofit. Additionally, many entrenched business and community spokespeople would raise objections to our vacating a building that was owned by one of the chamber's most important and influential members—Commerce Bank.

While there was some strong pushback on this idea, there was also great support from the likes of Mike Haverty, CEO of Kansas City Southern Railway, along with Tom McDonnell, CEO of DST Systems; Bob Regnier, CEO of Bank of Blue Valley; and Terry Dunn, CEO of JE Dunn Construction. Without their support and the support of other influential community leaders, this idea would have been dead on arrival.

After almost a year of discussions, debates, and outright disagreements (including many arrows shot in my direction), the day for the boards of the chamber and the Kansas City Area Development Council to vote on their respective resolutions finally arrived.

Over the course of the previous year, we had successfully changed the original narrative from saving an old train station to building a modern gathering place for the broader community. We created a vision: the station would house many of the community's social impact organizations. They could meet, work, and innovate in collaboration to better the community. Our vision enabled us to enlist the support of almost the entire community on both sides of the state line, which is no easy task. However, the vision alone was not enough. We had to deliver a clear, understandable, and compelling purpose while demonstrating to the community that we could successfully execute the plan.

At the chamber meeting, I invited final comments on the proposed resolution. Although I had counted heads prior to the meeting and knew that I had enough yes votes to carry the resolution, I still sat with nervous anticipation. My strong preference was that the vote be unanimous, or nearly unanimous, to demonstrate that even the early dissenters had come around and were now supportive. The boardroom was filled with tension.

The media waited eagerly outside the boardroom to hear the results. Finally, after discussion and debate concluded, I called for the final vote. The resolution easily passed. The board members broke into applause, realizing that they had not only taken a vote to preserve a regional and national treasure; they had taken a vote to come together as a community.

Collectively, we created a central gathering place for the community's business leadership and social impact organizations. The future of Kansas City's historic Union Station was assured, and the place had a new and exciting mission to fulfill. The relocation of the chamber's offices to help save Union Station turned out to be a huge community success. Along with the chamber, the Kansas City Area Development Council, the Kansas City Area Life Sciences Institute, Kansas City Election Board, and UMKC professional development are housed within the office environment. I consider the stewarding of this vision one of my most important and enduring contributions to the Kansas City community.

By the end of my term as chair of the chamber, the community had coalesced around the strategic plan and the Big 5. The actual implementation would be left to my successor and friend, Greg Graves, the CEO of Burns & McDonnell.

I remember when Greg called to ask me to chair the strategy to make Kansas City America's most entrepreneurial city. Perhaps this was a bit of payback since I was the one who strongly advocated for that initiative to be included in the Big 5. Although I really wanted to say no—I was worn out after my year as chair and with lots happening at UMB—I eventually said yes.

The first stop along the journey was to meet with Carl Schramm, CEO of the Ewing Marion Kauffman Foundation. Started in 1966 by Ewing Marion Kauffman, the founder of Marion Laboratories, the foundation had assets of over $3.5 billion. According to their website, the foundation's work "helps unlock opportunity for all so that people can achieve financial stability, upward mobility and economic prosperity—regardless of race, gender or geography."

This meeting was a watershed moment for me in terms of the Big 5 initiative and my leadership perspective, particularly about casting a captivating vision. The one thing I knew was that we were going to need the foundation's help if we had any chance of making this strategy a reality.

Carl, who was not a native of Kansas City, had a global perspective and was one of the foremost thinkers on how to create effective entrepreneurial ecosystems. He was now living in our community. He was quick to note that while Kansas City had a strong entrepreneurial past, the current situation was not strong. No comprehensive entrepreneurial ecosystem was currently in place.

Entrepreneurial ecosystems comprise people, culture, trust, and collaboration, but they are not spontaneous. It can take years, if not decades, of thoughtful planning and cultivation to create an ecosystem. Typical dimensions include leadership, access to capital, the flow of information, support, human capital, markets, and, of course, many, many entrepreneurs.

I asked Carl for his recommendation on how to jump-start the transformation. He had many good ideas, including a pledge of resources and financial support from the Kauffman Foundation. One thing, however, especially caught my attention. Carl said, "The first thing you need to do is to declare to the world that Kansas City is America's most entrepreneurial city."

What? Was he kidding?

I told Carl that I could not make that claim. I had no way to back it up. The data would not support the assertion. How could I make this declaration when places like Silicon Valley, Boston, and Austin had far more fact-based evidence in that regard than Kansas City?

Carl told me not to worry. He advised me to focus on the big picture and create an exciting, aspirational image of where we wanted to be, not where we currently were. It was a matter of focusing on the assets we had, not the ones we needed to build. He said no one would call me out on it: "Just declare it," he said, "and then build a comprehensive plan to fill in the gaps." This was not to be an initiative. It was to be a movement.

As much as I respected Carl, I was not convinced. I was worried about my own credibility. As someone who prides himself on using facts and data to back up his assertions, I was quite uncomfortable with this approach.

I sought out the advice of other respected leaders in the community, including Terry Dunn, CEO of JE Dunn Construction; Cliff Illig, founder of Cerner Corporation; Don Hall, CEO of Hallmark; and Jim Heeter, who was the current CEO of the chamber. Some thought it was a great idea to declare Kansas City as the most entrepreneurial city and own the claim, while others, like me, were more cautious. I thought about watering down the claim, but that would defeat the purpose. In the end, I decided to go for it. I would make the claim while simultaneously working aggressively to back it up.

The day came when it was time to declare the vision to the Kansas City community. I was extremely nervous and apprehensive. The event was held in the auditorium of the National World War I Museum and Memorial. Business, political, and community leaders were in attendance, along with the media. While I had already resolved to stake the claim and had worked with others to develop an outline of the plan to get us there, I still felt like we were getting way too far out over our skis.

The reaction to my remarks was amazing. The community responded with tremendous enthusiasm and support for the claim. There was great pride in being so aggressive and not taking a backseat to any other community. Although all the attendees knew we were not there yet, they were excited that someone was willing to take the leadership role and inspire the community to get us there. The days when residents were shy about Kansas City were coming to an end. The community was beginning to get its swagger back, even as a transformation was underway at UMB.

Over the next few years, the community worked diligently to address the shortcomings of our entrepreneurial ecosystem and made amazing progress. Today, it is not uncommon to see Kansas City in the top echelon of rankings of the most entrepreneurial communities in America. I take some pride in that accomplishment.

I look fondly on this experience in terms of how it positively affected the community's economic health and respectfully acknowledge the leadership lessons I took from it. I came to appreciate afresh the transformative power of creating a compelling vision, articulating and communicating that vision to others, and enlisting others in the attainment of that vision. Although I wasn't completely comfortable putting forth a claim I couldn't yet factually support, I saw how the aspiring vision united and galvanized us all.

One of my favorite sayings, often used by Nelson Mandela and attributed to author Joel Barker, is "Vision without action is merely a dream. Action without vision is merely passing time. But vision and action can change the world." In this case, we successfully developed the vision, the strategies, and the actions necessary to move the ball forward. The combination of those three variables became one powerful force.

Leadership is about creating the conditions in which others can thrive and succeed. In this case, I articulated the vision and enlisted others more capable than I in the project. I did not have the requisite skills to undertake the necessary initiatives by myself, but others working collaboratively did. It was no different from how I was able to bring together the group of Fidelity associates to research and resolve that long-standing tax dispute with the IRS so many years ago.

One of my principles is that it is always better to do something than do nothing. In this situation we could have just stood around, taken stock of our situation, and said that there was little we could do about it. Instead, we did something bold, engaged the community in our goals, and took prudent risks. That made all the difference.

My job was to lead, motivate, and provide support and encouragement to those much more qualified than I to act and complete the roadmap. When I needed help or needed to assemble a group, it was easy to do because of the strong relationships I had built over the previous years. But that was only one part of the picture. Once there was a clear, aspirational vision that others could rally behind, individuals and groups started to sprout up spontaneously all over the region in support of the movement. These groups included KCSourceLink, 1 Million Cups, Kauffman Founders School, LaunchKC, the Kansas City Startup Village, and more. The energy behind this movement was palpable. This entire experience became a bright and meaningful element on my mosaic.

On March 22, 2011, Sylvester "Sly" James became the fifty-fourth mayor of Kansas City, Missouri, the city's second African American mayor. Sly was in the race against local attorney Mike Burke. The race had been cordial, with participants agreeing early on not to use personal attacks against each other. This was a breath of fresh air in an otherwise acrimonious national political environment. Sly won with 54 percent of the vote.

Sly had grown up on Kansas City's East Side and graduated from Bishop Hogan High School. He honorably served his country in the US Marines and later attended Rockhurst College, where he secured a Bachelor of Arts in English. He graduated from the University of Minnesota Law School in 1983 with his Juris Doctor.

I became friends with Sly in the months leading up to the election and supported his bid for the office. He endeared himself to me with his wit, wisdom, and genuine care for all the people of Kansas City. He was passionate about making Kansas City a better place to live and work. So was I. Sly was a Democrat, and I was a Republican, but that didn't matter to me or to him. The more local a race is, the less parties and politics matter. Competence and the ability to get things done are the key factors. Sly had both.

Soon after his election, Sly asked me to co-chair his mayoral transition committee with three other notable Kansas Citians. Although I have always had a political bent, and I genuinely liked Sly as a person and as a politician, I did not want to do this. I was already up to my eyeballs with my work at UMB, was leading the effort to make Kansas City America's most entrepreneurial city, and still involved with other community projects. However, I couldn't say no. Sly was a friend. Even more important, I wanted his time as mayor to get off to a good start. If he thought I could be helpful to him, I was all in.

At the first transition team meeting, the group decided that the city needed a long-term cohesive strategy and plan, a future roadmap with a multidimensional scorecard to measure progress. We set out to create that. It took dozens of meetings with many constituencies over six weeks to develop, vet, and finalize a plan that the mayor could take with him to city hall.

There were many components to the plan, including a focus on renewing critical city infrastructure, revitalization of the city's East Side, better transportation alternatives, a focus on the root causes of crime, enhanced educational resources for the city's students, and a plan for the continued revitalization of downtown.

While we had a solid strategic plan, Sly recognized that one of the missing ingredients was positive culture—resident pride in Kansas City.

Like most of us, he was tired of hearing the comparisons to other like cities such as Nashville, Austin, Denver, and Indianapolis—cities that were growing more quickly, had better branding behind them, and were further along in their redevelopment. These cities had somehow stolen the limelight from Kansas City.

The years of implementing the plan under Sly's leadership were full of challenges, with notable successes and some disappointments. There was the success of the downtown streetcar line, the approval by voters of a new single-terminal airport, the continued revitalization of downtown, the opening of a new city-owned supermarket in a former food desert, numerous infrastructure improvements, a new convention center hotel, and the launch of Turn the Page KC, a nonprofit created to improve third grade reading proficiency.

Someone looked back at the scorecard from Sly's eight years in office and tabulated that the mayor had achieved sixteen of his eighteen goals. Two of the notable disappointments were 1) the inability to get approval of an east-west extension of the streetcar line and 2) the rejection by the voters of the mayor's pre-K proposal, which would have enacted a new sales tax for ten years to generate funding for free pre-K programs.

In an interview with Channel 41 KSHB at the close of his second term, Mayor James said these words.

> Nobody liked Kansas City, and we were always comparing ourselves to other places, wishing we could be St. Louis—always feeling inferior. And now, after having those feelings, now we're recognizing that we're pretty damn nice. And we're wearing KC on everything. We got a little giddy-up in our step. We've won some ball games. We're on the map. They're putting us on TV on the soccer games. We've got a streetcar that other cities come to see. We're building stuff. We've got a new airport terminal coming in. We're addressing situations on the East Side. We're trying to work with kids and all of that. Which of those two feelings is better?

I took great satisfaction in helping to fashion a forward-looking strategy for the city and helping the mayor set the community on an exciting new trajectory over his two terms in office.

Michelle and I absolutely loved our time in Kansas City and were proud of the contributions we made. During the twelve years we lived there, we became involved, in one way or another, in almost every significant community service organization. There were innumerable events to attend, events to sponsor, and fundraising projects in pursuit of a kinder, more giving, and diverse Kansas City.

Between my work at UMB and our work in the community, Michelle and I often found ourselves exhausted. Once I took my daughter Christine to a gala at the Kansas City Zoo to give Michelle a well-deserved break. Another time I took my nephew Norman, who happened to be in town, to the Symphony Ball. Despite the hectic pace, Michelle and I were proud of our role in helping make Kansas City a better place to live and work. Together I estimate that we helped raise more than $100 million for various community organizations and projects.

Michelle and I raised our daughters in Kansas City. We moved there when Christine was about to enter the sixth grade and Sarah was about to enter the third grade. Both graduated from high school in Kansas City before heading out to college. In general, they thrived there with lots of friends and activities. However, they both treasured their summers on Cape Cod.

I like to think that we all learned and adopted core Midwestern values from our time there. We had fun at our Weatherby Lake house where we made lifelong friends. Even today, we still miss friends and colleagues and the charm of that great American city. Most important, it introduced us to another part of America. We came to appreciate the humility and can-do attitude of Midwesterners.

Having lived in the Greater Boston area, Cincinnati, Kansas City, and St. Louis, and traveled to most parts of the country, I have come to appreciate that there is much more that unites us than divides us. In these times of division in our country, I wish more Americans could experience how the other half lives. I am confident that this would bring us closer together. After all, we are all Americans.

My time in Kansas City was a time of accelerated personal and professional growth. Many of the principles presented in this book were developed or refined there. My mosaic blossomed through my interactions with thousands of individuals, each adding a unique contribution. From riding a horse down Main Street during the annual American Royal Cattle Drive and driving a NASCAR car at 150 mph around the Kansas Speedway to learning how to hunt, my time in Kansas City opened my eyes to the beauty and wonders of the Midwest and its people. I am a more well-balanced leader and person as a result.

One of the most profound takeaways from that time was a new understanding about the intersection of business and community. It takes businesses to make a community, and it takes a community to make businesses. The two are inextricably linked. I came to realize the responsibility of business leaders to give back: in monetary terms and in terms of time, talent, and resources.

By virtue of the elevated position that businesses occupy within a community, businesses must be strong proponents of needed social change inside and outside their organizations' walls. All companies serve multiple stakeholders, including shareholders, customers, associates, suppliers, and their communities. In August 2019, the Business Roundtable, a national association of CEOs of America's leading companies, redefined the purpose of a corporation to be more inclusive and to promote "an economy that serves all Americans." After all, one of the best social impact programs is to provide employment to all those who seek it. This statement seems like a step in the right direction.

Before my time at UMB, I had not thought much about being a social impact leader. I did what I thought was expected of me as a business leader. I went to Kansas City as the "inside guy" never expecting to be a community leader. During my years there, however, I came to realize the power of leveraging a business platform for social good. I left there a much stronger advocate for those less fortunate. I learned to use my platform for good in Kansas City. I found my voice as a community leader.

The two roles following my time at UMB did not require the level of civic leadership that was required of me in Kansas City. The circumstances in those jobs were completely different, as you'll discover in the following chapters. In both cases, the roles turned out to have unexpectedly short tenures. Still, Michelle and I embraced the communities in which we lived and did our best to make them better places. Although our community roles were more curtailed, my belief in the power of an executive platform for social good remained strong. That belief was one of the driving factors in shaping the third chapter of my life.

> **Notable Cause in Kansas City**
>
> I remember the day that David Byrd, the relatively new president of the YMCA of Greater Kansas City, walked into my office at UMB. I immediately liked David and knew that we would be partners. Later, I encouraged him to stop and look across Grand Boulevard, and asked, "What do you see there?"
>
> David saw, as most did, a nearly empty parking lot.
>
> I asked David to close his eyes and imagine a vibrant space filled with people of all ages coming and going at all hours of the day to take advantage of the daycare, pool, and workout facilities, or afterschool programming and recreational activities. Everyone was laughing as they entered and exited the building.
>
> This is what I envisioned, and I wanted to know if David could see it too. Because he could, we began a partnership to conceive and build a new downtown Kansas City YMCA.
>
> We created pictures and videos of a new vibrant YMCA, detailing how it would enhance the downtown community. We went to numerous

meetings to enlist others in our vision. Without a vision that captured the spirit of a new day, this project would never have gotten off the ground.

As with any large project, we had roadblocks to overcome. The most significant emerged when a group of senior community leaders proposed rehabilitating an underutilized old theater in the downtown core as the site. At first, David and I rejected the idea.

Neither of us were excited about rehabilitating another old building. I had seen how difficult that was with Union Station. It became clear that this was the will of a group of important community leaders who believed we could kill two birds with one stone. We could rehabilitate a decaying community asset and get a new YMCA in downtown Kansas City. It took me some time, but eventually I saw the wisdom of their idea. It was far more important that the project get done than where it got done.

The project turned out to be far more complex than we originally envisioned. It took seven-plus years, much longer than either of us had expected, to raise the funds, choose the final site, renovate the building, and navigate the complexities of the COVID-19 pandemic. There were days when David and I were discouraged, but we held each other up and pressed on. It takes patience and persistence to accomplish meaningful things.

On June 7, 2021, to the excitement of residents, visitors, politicians, and community advocates, the new Kirk Family YMCA opened downtown. It was a great day.

Shortly before leaving Kansas City, Michelle and I were recognized by Starlight Theatre with their annual Star Award for community service. The evening, with our daughters in attendance, was memorable. It seemed Michelle and I had made a difference in the lives of Kansas Citians. That meant a lot to us.

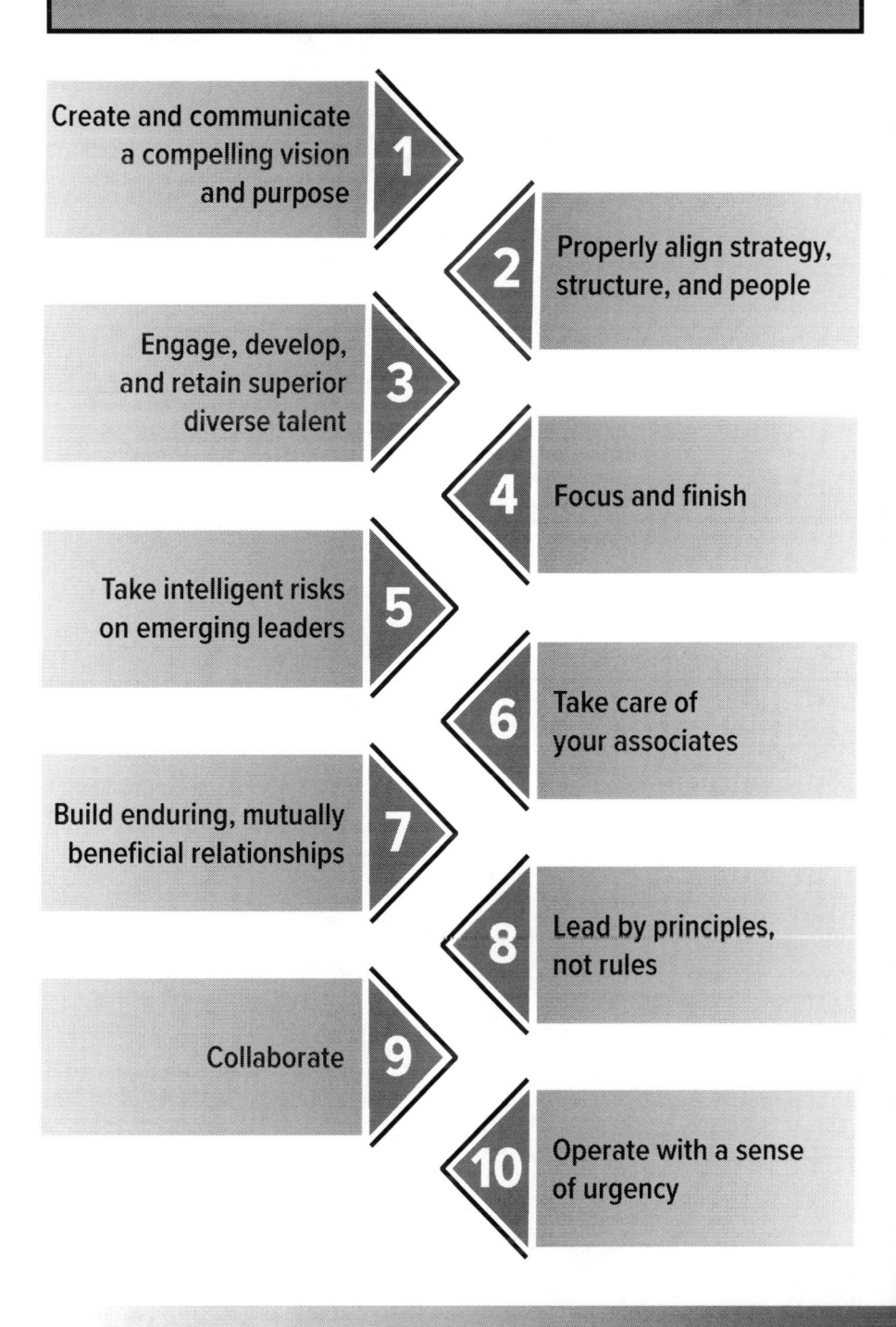

10 Life and Leadership Principles

1. Create and communicate a compelling vision and purpose
2. Properly align strategy, structure, and people
3. Engage, develop, and retain superior diverse talent
4. Focus and finish
5. Take intelligent risks on emerging leaders
6. Take care of your associates
7. Build enduring, mutually beneficial relationships
8. Lead by principles, not rules
9. Collaborate
10. Operate with a sense of urgency

10 Life and Leadership Principles from My Seat at the Table

1. Create and communicate a compelling vision and purpose

Vision without action is merely a dream.
Action without vision just passes the time.
Vision with action can change the world.
– JOEL A. BARKER, author and motivational speaker

Creating, communicating, and executing a compelling vision is the most important role a leader plays. That said, the world is dynamic. A successful leader recognizes the constant need to reevaluate an organization's direction as the external environment shifts and changes. Throughout my career, I have been fortunate to work alongside visionary CEOs. Each of them painted broad and compelling pictures of a future desired state. Only then did they put forth aspirational images that individuals and teams wanted to be part of and help build. At the outset, the leaders didn't have all the answers as to how to get where they wanted to go. They did have the wisdom to know that clearly imparting their vision and purpose and enlisting others in that purpose was the first step.

2. Properly align strategy, structure, and people

Hope is not a strategy.
But having a clear and actionable strategy gives one hope.
– PdS

Undertake the hard work to create a clear, aspirational, and applicable strategy *before* deciding what organizational structure and leadership competencies are needed to ensure successful execution. Once the strategy is firm, you can choose the best structure from the available options. Know that there is no such thing as a perfect organizational structure, only an array of alternatives, each with their respective strengths and weaknesses. Only after the strategy and structure are firmly in place can you select the right talent. Proper strategy and structure inform the skills, abilities, roles, expertise, and experiences necessary to successfully execute the strategy. The only way to make an inherently flawed organizational structure work is to have individuals collaborate under a common purpose. Do not make the mistake of choosing strategy, structure, and people in reverse order. I've seen many teams come in front of leadership and boards with completed organization design plans and talent already selected before the strategy has even been set. This creates a misalignment among strategy, structure, and people.

3. Engage, develop, and retain superior diverse talent

Not everything that counts can be counted,
and not everything that can be counted counts.
– WILLIAM BRUCE CAMERON, sociologist

The war for talent is today's most pressing strategic and leadership challenge. Be prepared to fight the talent wars on multiple fronts. Many different and flexible approaches are required, from harvesting new talent and developing key talent to retaining existing talent. In today's fast-paced environment, it is imperative that leaders take a contemporary view of the talent marketplace. Today's associates work differently than those in the past. They don't work less hard or fewer hours; they just work differently. With the advent of technology that fully enables remote work for many roles, employers must adjust or fall behind the pack. Trust your associates to engage in their craft but on terms that are good for the employer *and* the associate. Engagement is critical; create the conditions and build trust with your associates so they are able to bring their best selves to work every day. Remember that diversity, in all its forms, creates a stronger, more fulfilling, and successful workplace and society.

4. Focus and finish

A great strategy poorly executed is doomed to failure,
while a good strategy flawlessly executed will win every time.
– PdS

No organization can succeed with competing agendas, priorities, individuals, and teams. Lack of focus leads to a fundamental misalignment between strategy and action, which leads to waste, conflict, inefficiency, and ultimately failure. When an organization fully focuses its energy and resources on completing initiatives and actions that advance shared vision and goals, organizations and people flourish.

5. Take intelligent risks on emerging leaders

Near failure is a far better teacher than actual failure.
– PdS

Great leaders understand their obligation to build the next generation of talent. They provide emerging and experienced leaders with abundant opportunities to learn and grow. Present your rising stars with challenging and/or difficult situations just beyond their current skill level. These experiences, along with skillful coaching, will accelerate the growth process. Strong leaders build fences around key talent to give them room to roam but protect them from unnecessary danger. Enlightened leaders allow their aspiring leaders to approach the fence, then gently pull them back when they sense danger. This approach provides nearly all the learning associated with actual failure without enduring damaging outcomes, including possible irreparable damage to the emerging leader's career.

6. Take care of your associates

If you take care of associates, they will take care of clients, and the rest will take care of itself.
– PdS

If you treat associates as respected partners or colleagues, regardless of level, you will receive far more committed associates in return. I choose to use the word *associate* in this book over *employee* because of the important distinction between the two words. An employee is a person employed for wages or salary, especially at a nonexecutive level, while an associate is a partner or colleague in business or at work. Which of these would you rather be? No matter what the level of the position, associates beat employees every time.

7. Build enduring, mutually beneficial relationships

Even in today's highly digitally-led world, genuine, authentic, and mutually beneficial relationships remain the cornerstone of human thriving.
– PdS

Relationships can be characterized as either transactional or mutually beneficial. Transactional relationships can be defined as "You do something for me, and I will do something for you" for a defined time, task, or remuneration. For example, you work for me, and I give you a paycheck. Enduring relationships, on the other hand, are characterized by a commitment from both parties to foster a long-term, mutually beneficial relationship characterized by trust. These relationships achieve "relationship equilibrium," in which one gives as much as one gets back. To be successful, leaders need enduring, mutually beneficial relationships at all levels, inside and outside their organizations. The higher the leader's level, the more important it is to have enduring relationships across multiple spheres.

8. Lead by principles, not rules

*Always do what is right, not what is popular at the moment.
No matter the cost.*
— R. Crosby Kemper Jr.

Principles define the parameters for appropriate action while rules seek to constrain creativity and innovation. For example, contrast the US Declaration of Independence versus the Code of Hammurabi. The former is a highly principled document while the latter comprises 282 discrete rules. The code is now a relic of history while the Declaration of Independence has been emulated the world over. Principled leaders set appropriate guardrails and support mechanisms to get the best performance out of their teams and organizations. Leading by principles is a much more enlightened way of managing organizations and teams in the twenty-first century. Today's associates expect to have the freedom to act when within well-established and understood boundaries.

9. Collaborate

*It's amazing what can be accomplished
when you do not care who gets the credit.*
— Harry S. Truman

If you want to accelerate positive results, check your ego at the door, collaborate with others, and share the credit. Singleness of purpose and a genuine willingness to collaborate are essential ingredients to individual and team success. Another essential ingredient is humility. Your humility allows others to rise and shine in the moment. While some speak of teamwork as the highest form of collective activity, I prefer to speak of collaboration, which requires a level of commitment beyond any single moment or situation. It requires a willingness to practice self-sacrifice for the good of the whole. Accomplishing great things requires "one dream, one team."

10. Operate with a sense of urgency

> *The way to get started is to quit talking and begin doing.*
> – WALT DISNEY

Your baseline operating paradigm should be to lead with urgency. History, data, analysis, and reason are essential ingredients when making decisions. So, too, are time and intuition. Take measured and prudent risks within the context of well-articulated boundaries and appropriate measures of success. If you are comfortable—even if the worst possible outcome were to occur—it is time to act. Use your common sense, intuition, and empirical analysis to make good, informed, and timely decisions. If for some reason you make a wrong decision, nimbly correct course. People won't remember that you started off on the wrong course; they'll remember where you ended up.

Chapter 7

The Evolving Crisis of Leadership: A Trifecta of Pressures

Home ownership is one of the surest ways for individuals and families to create and sustain wealth. The benefits of home ownership include building equity as the mortgage is paid down (assuming the value of the home either stays constant or increases over time), controlling the monthly cost of housing, building credit, and being a fixed part of a community. The US government has made the expansion of home ownership a priority for many years through policies like the mortgage interest deduction, which makes the cost of home ownership advantageous versus other forms of shelter. It was against this backdrop that in 1994 Congress created a national objective to increase home ownership from roughly 64% to 67.5% of US households by the year 2000.

Throughout the first seven years of the new decade, a general decline in the standards that banks and other financial institutions applied when approving credit accelerated. Interest rates had been held artificially low for an extended period, making it difficult for banks to earn spread income (the difference between the rate a bank pays to gather deposits and the interest rate at which it loans money out). Banks and other financial institutions developed more and more products that would put more Americans in homes, thus helping to support the objective of increasing home ownership.

There were, however, serious unintended consequences, including a huge cost to families and society at large.

Alongside the main street banks, the Wall Street banks developed an entirely new category of synthetic securities (mostly derivative) securities. With such products, the value of the security is "derived" from another related security or basket of securities. These highly complex products, when packaged and sold, allowed risk to be transferred to unsuspecting buyers all over the world with near cataclysmic results.

As time progressed, credit standards deteriorated even further. For example, a category of mortgage loans called subprime loans became a prominent fixture in the mortgage marketplace. These loans were made to some of the riskiest borrowers, those who did not meet the traditional credit underwriting standards known as the 5Cs: capital, collateral, capacity, conditions, and character (See stand-alone box on p. 125).

Some mortgage loans were even labeled low-documentation loans; others were called no-documentation loans. This category of loans was affectionately known throughout the industry as liar's loans. This alone should have been a clue that standards were slipping to unacceptably low levels.

There were also negative-amortization loans, in which the outstanding principal actually *increased* with each payment. Imagine your dismay if you discovered that you had taken out one of these loans. Finally, loans were issued at low, introductory teaser rates that, when adjusted to current market rates, became unaffordable to the borrower. The objective was to keep the monthly payment as low as possible and not worry about the outstanding amount of the loan.

An underlying assumption was terribly flawed—the belief that the value of homes (the collateral) would always rise and never fall. Lenders who thought this way assumed that the collateral would more than cover the amount of the debt if the buyer failed to pay the mortgage. Rather than rely on the capacity of the borrower to service the debt, these lenders were relying on the liquidation value of the collateral to make them whole in the event of default. In practice, lenders were violating at least two of the standard 5 Cs of credit: capacity and collateral.

This phenomenon was not limited to consumer credit. The same deterioration was occurring in commercial lending, especially in commercial real estate. Here, stiff competition between lenders was driving down the standards for approval. For example, instead of only making loans for 80 percent of appraised value, a bank might make a loan with a 100 percent loan-to-value ratio. This left no room to recoup the loan's principal if the value of the real estate fell, which, of course, it did. This was the state of the marketplace during my role as president and chief operating officer of UMB Financial Corporation.

As the quality of loans in the marketplace continued to deteriorate, we at UMB were beginning to see the contours of the upcoming crisis. We were finding it difficult to compete for loans as many of our competitors were making what we deemed to be imprudent loans without proper credit underwriting. We could not get comfortable with the credit decisions that other banks were making. As a result, our growth rate was lower than many of our peers. We could not know exactly when the crisis would occur, but we became increasingly convinced that it would. It became a matter of when, rather than if.

The UMB leadership team faced constant pressure to adjust its business model to seek quicker, more dramatic gains. UMB was even portrayed by some as doing a disservice to investors and communities by not participating in subprime lending or other practices that were yielding premiums. We faced pressure to provide access to loans to almost anyone who walked through our door. The decision to adhere to the long-held conservative business model rather than chase lucrative fads did not make UMB the envy of Wall Street, at least not yet.

At UMB we held strongly to our historical credit standards, which effectively hampered our growth as our clients and prospects found looser terms elsewhere. The temptation to join the crowd was hard to resist, but resist we did. It was because of UMB's long-term approach and time-tested principles that we avoided and then successfully navigated the crisis.

Why did leaders in other financial services companies fail to do the same? Why did our nation have a subprime crisis that in its most basic form was a violation of some basic principles? The answer is complex because human behavior is involved.

The simple answer is greed, but there's nothing new about greed. Largely, the cause behind this crisis lay in the fact that there was no rule or law that said that subprime loans could not be made. New products had been created that seemed too good to be true, and there was a tremendous amount of money to be made. A concentration of organizations and individuals succumbed to pressures related to achieving immediate or outsized results.

One of the strongest patterns in my personal leadership mosaic is my principle number eight: a commitment to lead by principles rather than rules or laws. Crosby Kemper Jr. and the other leaders at UMB held this same commitment long before I came on the scene. Fortunately, we were aligned and agreed to lead by principles. The underlying assumption was that you cannot legislate ethics.

Throughout the ages, a mix of principles and rules has been developed to guide human behavior. Millions of individual rules have been written in attempts to prescribe proper behavior. Some rules are written while others are dictated by an implied understanding. These rules attempt to set the parameters for societal actions by imposing firm expectations with specific consequences for non-adherence.

Understandably, we are all subjected to a mix of principles and rules throughout our lifetime. Some we follow religiously, others we do not. From an organizational standpoint, when presented with such real-life scenarios as opportunity, mediocrity, and crisis, the influence of leadership weighs heavily on how principles and rules are used and balanced.

5 Cs of Credit

The 5 Cs of credit are the time-tested standards by which banks and other financial institutions examine the creditworthiness of a potential consumer or commercial borrower. They are capital, collateral, capacity, conditions, and character. Here is a brief overview.

Capital: Capital represents the total amount of assets invested. Having a strong capital position enables borrowers to withstand sudden shocks either to their own condition or the external environment. Borrowers (companies or individuals) with low capital levels typically represent a higher credit risk to the lender.

Collateral: Collateral is the asset that a company or an individual pledges to secure the loan. Collateral can take many forms, including cash, securities, the title to a building, certain equipment, a life insurance policy, an automobile, and other hard assets that can be liquidated in the event the borrower defaults on the loan. Lenders don't want to liquidate the collateral to get repaid because there is no certainty as to the value of the collateral at the time it needs to be sold. The liquidation of collateral can be very messy and is always the last resort.

Capacity: Capacity is a measurement of the ability to repay the loan from regular, predictable cash flows and other sources of income. Lenders want to see that there is enough ongoing capacity to ensure repayment. Certain financial ratios are used to determine and monitor borrower capacity.

Conditions: Conditions are the specifics of any transaction, including the principal amount, interest rates, and any guarantors that might be required to strengthen the loan. Conditions also consider the health of the economy, unemployment, and other external conditions.

Character: Character is a comprehensive assessment of an individual or company's track record of paying back prior loans, even if events turn negative. Character can be assessed in quantitative and qualitative terms. A lender can look at credit reports, repayment history, and other quantitative elements to determine the likelihood that an individual or business will repay a debt. The qualitative assessment of an individual's willingness to repay a loan even when the chips are down is extremely

> important. This is the real character part of the assessment. In my view, this is the most important of the 5 Cs. Many loans that meet the other criteria will be turned down based on concerns about character alone, as they should be. However, some loans that fall short on the quantitative analysis of the 5C's may be approved based upon the borrower's high character, reputation and prior repayment history.

Having had a front row seat to principled leadership at UMB, I've spent many hours considering the contrast between those leaders and others who clearly failed ethical standards and good business practices. What was dominant in their personal mosaics that led to such failure?

I wanted to understand what happens when leaders with individual mosaics come together within an organizational context. How do leaders influence the ethical framework of others? What result does that influence have on the cultural environment and decision-making framework?

I've identified several forces that can challenge and compromise leadership. These include the desire for expediency, unrealistic performance expectations, and personal aspirations.

Expediency. We live in a fast-paced world in which patience is considered more of a character flaw than a virtue. Leaders engage in real-time communication and quick decision making just to keep pace. In our technology-led society, there is also an expectation that any task can and should be completed extremely quickly.

The business landscape is littered with examples of people and organizations striving for expediency. Stories of people trying to make a fast buck abound. The scenario of a company's new CEO taking over and quickly cutting costs, compromising associates, abandoning the community, and then selling the organization at a handsome premium to get an exorbitant payday is sadly familiar. The desire for expediency can compromise a leader's ethical framework to achieve a short-term outcome. Not everyone will be take the shortcut approach, but many will be tempted.

Unrealistic performance expectations. The push for expediency and short-term profits can lead to relentless pressure to perform. Limits on personal and organizational performance are constantly being stretched—leading to pressure to get better, move quicker, and deliver stronger results. In an organizational context, leaders regularly conduct assessments of how much risk is reasonable to achieve a certain performance level. An old axiom touts "the greater the risk, the greater the reward." While the axiom holds true, its reverse holds true as well: The greater the risk, the larger the potential loss.

In performance-oriented cultures, leaders are naturally tempted to take outsized risks. Their jobs and remuneration depend upon it. This expectation of superior performance at any cost was a contributing factor to the financial crisis.

Personal aspiration. We all have cherished aspirations, ranging from the desire to be a good parent to wanting to climb Mount Everest. Although it would be difficult to find a shortcut to success in either of these cases, some people might try. For example, Rosie Ruiz's desire to be first over the finish line at the eighty-fourth Boston Marathon drove her to extreme behavior. Here's a description from a July 1980 article in *Running Times* magazine:

> Apparently, Ruiz had dropped out of the race, hopped on the subway, got off about a mile from the finish line, and ran in from there.
>
> While Ruiz was initially recognized as the winner, she was later stripped of the title following an investigation by the Boston Athletic Association. Not only did her personal aspirations ruin her reputation, she stole the well-deserved glory from the real winner.

When kept in perspective, personal aspirations are, of course, healthy. When those aspirations get out of hand, however, they can challenge a person's moral compass. While plenty of lenders at all levels knew that loans that seemed too good to be true were, in fact, not good for the borrower, their aspirations may have driven them to ignore the voice of their conscience. They might have reasoned that there are no laws (rules) against these types of loans.

The following chart depicts the relationship between rules and principles and how the forces of expediency, performance, and personal aspirations create tension between principles and rules. As shown at the bottom, effective leadership must balance these opposing forces and the tension that they create.

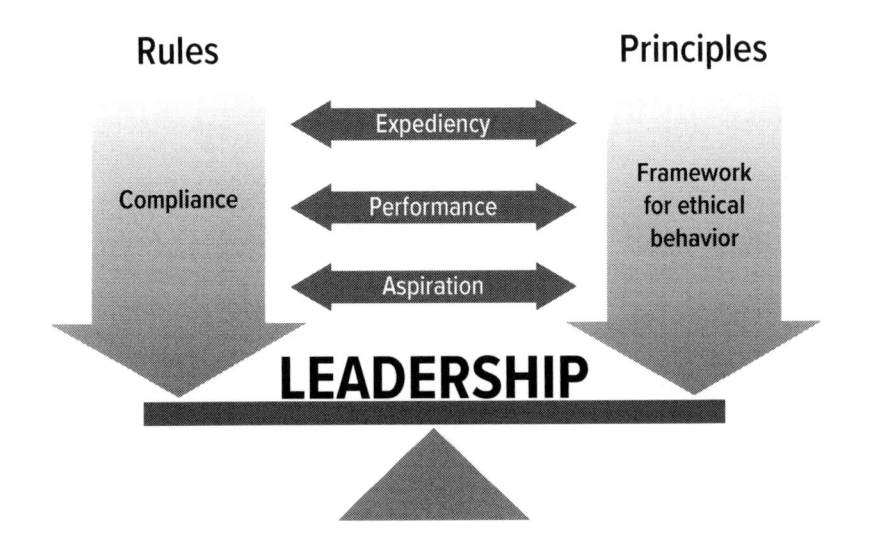

Rules — Compliance

Principles — Framework for ethical behavior

Expediency

Performance

Aspiration

LEADERSHIP

Undeterred by forces related to expediency, unrealistic performance expectations, or aspiration, UMB leadership and the board of directors concluded that while the company would have increased earnings in the short term by participating in the subprime lending phenomenon, the longer-term health of the organization was more important than short-term profits. There was also an expectation that the house of cards—subprime mortgages and risky loans—was not sustainable and would eventually fall with devastating consequences. The leadership team chose to remain dedicated to its core constituents and to a set of core principles about what was right. This allowed UMB to come through the crisis stronger while failed banks across the continent unfortunately left behind the carnage of ruined lives and careers.

When it all came crashing down, there was plenty of blame to pass around. The federal government, regulators, Wall Street and Main Street bankers, rating agencies, the buyers of the synthetic securities, and yes, even the borrowers who were looking for an easy and affordable way to attain home ownership, had a hand in the collapse. All these entities broke the public trust that keeps our society together.

Additionally, the large investment banks (many later deemed "too big to fail") created even more new ways to spread the risk of the toxic loans. They packaged the substandard loans together and sold the packages to unsuspecting buyers, all while making millions of dollars for their services. When the unraveling of this excessive leverage began in 2007, a glaring lack of accountability and transparency among all the players became apparent. What may have been less apparent, but arguably just as important, was the role principled leadership *should have played* in avoiding such a demise of our national and global economy.

By September 17, 2008, the financial industry began to unravel. Lehman Brothers collapsed on September 15; the Reserve Primary Fund "broke the buck" the following day, collectively sending ripples through the entire global financial sector. The world's financial system essentially came to a halt. This triggered an escalation in money market mutual fund outflows, which caused short-term funding for businesses and municipalities to freeze. At the same time, interbank funding markets became locked while overnight rates reached extraordinarily high levels.

In other words, banks were not lending to one another because of the uncertainty as to the value of the underlying collateral. During those days, immense pressure was associated with each decision—any misstep could potentially lead to dire consequences beyond which any of the players had previously experienced.

The financial system was coming apart, so much so that the federal government quickly stepped in with several extraordinary programs to stabilize the system. The establishment of the Troubled Asset Relief Program (TARP) was largely considered to be the most controversial of these moves. TARP was established in part to inject additional capital into banking and financial institutions that were being forced to write down the value of mortgages and mortgage securities, which led to significant capital shortfalls. Without the creation of the TARP program, it is at least conceivable that the entire financial system could have collapsed.

When TARP was first created, the premise was that the strong banks—those with quality balance sheets and substantial capital levels—as well as the weaker banks should take the offer of cheap, temporary government capital. The regulators began pushing even the strongest banks to take the capital in an effort to show solidarity with the weaker institutions. Some stronger banks took the government up on their offer. We at UMB did not. Despite significant pressure from the regulators, UMB did not capitulate.

Over the ensuing weeks, UMB's board of directors had numerous conversations with senior UMB management regarding the TARP program. Were we tempted by the offer? No.

Even though the capital was offered at an attractive rate, UMB never seriously considered the offer. The leadership and the board always went back to the basic principle of doing what was right, not what was popular. This was one of Crosby Kemper Jr.'s guiding principles, and we all shared his commitment to this principle.

CEO Mariner Kemper lamented about how it was not right for those that did not need the capital to take it just so that they might be able to earn a few extra dollars. In the end, the decision to pass on TARP was a good one: the program quickly became tainted. Those banks that took TARP were viewed with great skepticism by the general public.

Temptation will always exist—and it can lead to catastrophe—as it did in this case. Did too many business and government leaders let us down as our economy slipped and collapsed? The answer is obvious: yes. What happened during the financial crisis could have been avoided if leaders had carefully weighed the forces of expediency, performance, and aspiration and chosen to follow a moral compass to do what was right. Given the magnitude of the economic crisis our nation experienced and the increasingly complex nature of society, there were clearly many instances in which leaders acted without regard for potential disastrous outcomes.

In 2009, following the unraveling of the US economy, leadership and top team consultant Robert J. Thomas wrote the following in *Talent Management* magazine:

> We hunger for ethical leaders. We want to be led by men and women who know what the right thing to do is and then actually do it. The evidence can be found in virtually every organization's survey of employee engagement. The highest scores routinely go to the men and women who can be relied upon to do what they say, who grasp the difference between legal and illegal—and who have the courage of their convictions to make difficult choices—even when those choices put their own well-being at risk.

The specifics as to which rules or principles each of us follow are as diverse as the mosaic frameworks we each possess. If you aspire to lead, you must adhere to the principles you hold true, remaining acutely aware of how they influence those around you and the core identity of the organization you represent. The betterment—or downfall—of your business, your community, and our society is at stake.

Chapter 8

Maintaining Perspective through Adversity:
Scottrade Financial Services

In early February 2016, I began the next phase of my career as president of Scottrade Financial Services in St. Louis. I was pleased to be returning to my roots in the brokerage and wealth management industry. This meant another uprooting, this time to the eastern side of Missouri. For the first time it would just be Michelle and me relocating; our daughters were off at college.

I chose the Scottrade opportunity for multiple reasons. I liked the idea of returning to the brokerage and investment businesses. I was impressed with Scottrade's value proposition and ethical approach to doing business. As an early adopter of the transformative potential of the internet, Scottrade's online trading platform was one of the best in the business. Rodger Riney, Scottrade's founder and CEO, believed, as I do, that the most important elements of running a successful enterprise are building trust and exceptional experiences for and between clients and associates.

While the business was generally performing well, the potential to accelerate growth at Scottrade excited me. The organization had recently started a nationally chartered bank and a registered investment advisor (RIA) to complement the core brokerage trading business. I thought we had a great opportunity to better leverage the various parts of the business. Clients were looking for a comprehensive offering from their provider, and we had the pieces to provide that kind of service. We just had to put our capabilities together and deliver them in a more integrated and seamless way.

Anyone meeting Rodger Riney immediately likes and respects him. He is a humble, classic American entrepreneur who built an incredible company from straightforward ideas about treating people, customers, and associates right and running a highly ethical organization. When others were still trying to determine what to do with the internet, Rodger had the foresight to enter the online discount brokerage trading business and to build a leading client trading platform. I knew that I could learn and grow from just being around him.

One of the benefits of joining Scottrade was that it allowed me to return to a private company. I never liked the exposure from being a senior executive of a public company. At Scottrade, details such as my compensation and the terms of my employment agreement would remain private. Additionally, being private meant that we could take the time we needed and allocate our capital in ways we thought would enhance the long-term growth prospects of the organization. I would not miss having to meet quarterly analyst targets and meeting with analysts every quarter to explain our results.

My sole concern in choosing Scottrade was that Rodger had recently gone public with his diagnosis of multiple myeloma, an aggressive form of cancer with about a 50 percent survival rate after five years. The company had no clear succession plan in place. I was concerned that Rodger might seek to sell the company if his health deteriorated.

We had a frank discussion about this. Rodger assured me that Scottrade was *his* company, his family's company, *his* baby. He had built the company from scratch and had no desire to part with it. He was focused on beating the disease and the competition. I was convinced.

Even as Rodger openly shared his health condition with me, I didn't revisit my decision to stay private about mine. As we were concluding one of our final interviews, Rodger mentioned that someone had told him that I also had some kind of a health condition. I instantly became nervous. I brushed the question off with a wave of my hand, saying, "Oh, it's nothing to be concerned about. I am fine."

This was my practiced response to such a question. I'd say something vague about an old injury or some other mild condition and promptly change the subject. I had no intention to put myself in a position where others might think less of me, or worse yet, think that I might not be up to the job at hand. I never meant to mislead; I only wanted to remain private about my health. Right or wrong, I felt that I needed to be a perceived as a strong leader, even a champion leader.

My predecessor had not been at the job for very long. He was a respected industry veteran, but he struggled with the Scottrade culture and his relationship with Rodger. He also had some differences of opinion about the strategic direction of the firm. In a private company, the owner/founder gets to set the rules. His departure had been messy and had left the organization shaken. There had been a long separation between his departure and my hiring.

Once I arrived, the meetings came fast and furious. Given that it had been some time since I was in the brokerage industry, the information flow was at first hard to assimilate. I quickly came to like and respect Rodger's executive leadership team (ELT). My direct reports were all quite capable but did not seem to be operating as a cohesive team. Also, I began to wonder how some of them might adjust to my leadership style and my expectations.

Initially, some of team members looked at me as a banker. They thought, What does he know about the discount brokerage industry? I would need to demonstrate to my new team and the ELT that my leadership skills would more than make up for any perceived or real lack of deep industry knowledge. Interestingly, I found myself in the same situation I was in when I showed up at UMB without a deep knowledge of banking. I would once again need to take the time to build credibility at all levels of the organization, including the board, by demonstrating that leadership skills were as important or more important than technical knowledge. I set out to do just that.

The first few months were challenging as I was still commuting between St. Louis and Kansas City, where Michelle was living. I spent quite a bit of time getting to know my leadership team and members of the ELT. I also needed to study to regain my credentials as a NASD Series 24 registered principal, which was no easy task.

Many important initiatives were already underway at the company, including planning for a full back-office conversion, efforts to accelerate growth in the core business while maintaining margins, and integrating our banking and registered investment advisor offerings. We were also anticipating launching a complete overhaul of our core trading capability, which was needed to keep pace with the competition.

One day, as I was reviewing letters and emails the organization sent to our clients, I was appalled that each department sent emails with its respective department name, most often unsigned. Each department's communication had its own look and feel. It was as if the correspondence was from completely different companies. These emails represented an organization that was operating in silos. Our internal organization structure was on display to our clients. I remember showing a few of these to Rodger. His directive was to fix it.

My key business partners were Kim Wells, the head of marketing; Chris McComish, the president of Scottrade Bank; Jane Wulf, our chief administrative officer; Drew Dennison, our CFO and COO; and Adym Rygmyr, our general counsel. We sat down together and agreed that we would all work in a "One Scottrade" approach. We would back-burner our individual objectives to pursue the broader, enterprise-wide objectives. We would move from loose cooperation to tight collaboration. We agreed to be one team in pursuit of one dream.

Clients don't care about the identity of the department serving them. It is all the same company to them. We agreed that no client should ever experience our company's internal organizational chart. Over the next few months, we and our respective teams collaborated to create a singular strategy that would allow us to present ourselves in the marketplace and to our associates as a cohesive organization.

By this point in my career, I had experienced all types of organizational approaches. There were functional, channel, geographic/regional, product, and many other structures. I had come to appreciate that a perfect organizational structure is a fantasy. That's not to say that there are not better or worse organizational structures, because there are. Structures that allow those closest to the client to have a voice make the most logical sense. Structures with limited bureaucracy—that vest individuals and teams with proper authority, accountability, and responsibility—work best. Structures that align around customers and customer segments allow for a more intimate knowledge of the client and are thus better when you are seeking client intimacy.

Even the best structure is not enough. To succeed, you need people who are humble enough to collaborate under a common purpose, strategy, and mission, and who are willing to self-sacrifice for the good of the whole. Shared goals, success measurements, and incentives in which everyone wins or loses together are essential. To put it succinctly, success is not in the structure; it is in the people and how they collaborate. It always has been and always will be this way.

A Short History of the Discount Brokerage Industry

It's interesting but maybe not surprising that the greatest organizations ever created to empower self-directed investors were created away from Wall Street. The eponymous Charles Schwab and Larry Waterhouse, Ned Johnson (Fidelity), Joe Ricketts (TD Ameritrade), and Rodger Riney (Scottrade) built their companies to challenge Wall Street hundreds and thousands of miles away from "The Street."

The staid, oligopolistic full-service brokerage business had been ripe for disruption with entrepreneurs from places like Boston, Omaha,

St. Louis, and San Francisco. Innovators in these places were not caught up in the hype of Wall Street—where so many believe that theirs is the only way. Wall Street had been the epicenter of American finance and capital markets almost since the country's founding. The entrepreneurs that built their companies away from Wall Street could envision a future business model built around technology, customer service, education, and empowerment even as the Wall Street players were hell-bent on maintaining the highly lucrative status quo.

These entrepreneurs lived and worked in places that gave them a decided advantage as the business environment began to change. They saw the world at ground level rather than from a high-rise office building in New York City. They asked some basic questions, including: Why does it cost $200 to trade one hundred shares of stock? Why can't individuals do their own research and investing? What value does the stockbroker add in the equation? What is the track record of brokers who are recommending stocks and receiving massive commissions? If individuals and brokers could be armed with the same information at the same time, would brokers be that much smarter? Could education be a substitute for broker services? Why is it that brokerage firms are so incredibly profitable?

As these questions circulated, it became clear that the end consumer was not getting a good deal under the Wall Street model. Several entrepreneurs, all at roughly the same time, determined there had to be a better way, a way that put the client rather than the broker at the center. With that, the self-directed investor emerged, and the nascent discount brokerage industry was about to explode. These firms worked tirelessly to level the playing field. Largely due to a superior value proposition, the discount brokerage industry would take market share from the full-service firms for the next thirty years.

The essence of the value proposition for the discount firms was this: *We will help you* (versus *We will do it for you*) or, said another way, *We'll do it with you, not for you.*

Home Depot was revolutionizing home improvement with their approach of "You can do it, we can help." Home Depot made it easy by

> providing support and education for millions of Americans to learn how to complete simple home repairs themselves. For example, they held seminars to teach Americans how to lay tile and do simple plumbing jobs.
>
> Similarly, the discount brokerage industry hosted thousands of conferences in hotel ballrooms to teach willing investors what they needed to know to take control of their investments. The idea that an individual had to fully delegate investment decisions to a full-service broker for high commissions began to fade away. Timely information, education, the internet, and easy-to-use technology was leveling the playing field. A new and better value proposition for many investors had arrived. With the middleman largely cut out, commission prices could be cut by as much as 90 percent (eventually this would become 100 percent as trading commissions fell to zero).
>
> The industry evolved over the years, but the basic premise that individuals could invest and trade on their own, unencumbered by a high-paid broker, remained. The full-service firms continually lost market share to these upstart firms and have never fully recovered.
>
> The advent of the internet allowed the discount industry to massively scale. Even today, there are new challengers to current incumbents, reframing the self-directed investor value proposition with new technology, products, services, and pricing conventions. Like others before them, Robinhood, Square, SoFi Invest, Acorns, Webull, Ally Invest, TradeStation, and others are altering the arc of the industry. Once again, not even one of these firms was spawned on Wall Street.

Although Scottrade was in the discount brokerage business, Rodger was convinced that strong relationships developed at the local level with capable people make a significant difference in acquiring clients and building the loyalty to retain those clients. As internet delivery of financial services was making personal service a thing of the past, this model stood out. While others in the industry didn't see having five hundred branches as an efficient use of human and financial capital, having a strong physical presence was nonnegotiable for Rodger. It was okay with him to reap the return on this business model down the road. It was also okay that the payback might be difficult to quantifiably measure with accuracy.

For example, it might seem difficult to justify the fact that Scottrade had two branches in Naples, Florida, while our competitors had one branch or no branch at all. Rodger understood something about Naples that our competitors didn't: Naples comprises two distinctly different parts, North Naples and downtown. Many residents do not access the other part of the community. They want to receive service in their local market. We retained both branches and enjoyed an outsized market share as a result.

Rodger used his intuition, instinct, knowledge of the client base and local markets, and his unshakable commitment to deliver a high-touch level of service to judge that we were better off with the network of branches than without it. The real value was not in the physical network itself but with the associates. Many of these branch associates were long-tenured and had great relationships with their clients. Although I largely agreed with Rodger about the number and placement of our branches, I was confident that we could do some trimming without doing significant harm to the client base.

If Scottrade were a public company, we might have been forced to consider a different approach in which near-term earnings might win against long-term client relationships. If we were a startup, like Robinhood, which has a very different business model, different client expectations, and a technology-only focused value proposition, our branch locations would not make sense. But we were neither public nor new. Millions of our clients had come to rely on our branch network, and we were not going to destroy it.

Shortly after I came on board, the leadership team, understanding that the extensive branch network would continue as a signature Scottrade feature, came together to launch a comprehensive strategic review. This resulted in a refreshed and forward-looking strategic plan to which we all committed. There was a lot of optimism about the future. However, we also had some company specific and significant industry specific issues that we needed to address.

Scottrade was undersized versus our larger competitors. At approximately $200 billion in assets, we were small in comparison to Fidelity, Schwab, and TD Ameritrade. Over time, size had become increasingly important in terms of achieving efficiencies and economies of scale. At the time, Fidelity was close to $5 trillion in assets and Schwab was close to $3 trillion in assets. We were closer to the size of E*TRADE (although they were double our size), another upstart that had captured a segment of the self-directed trading marketplace.

The core trading platform needed a top-to-bottom refresh. Our trading platform was significantly outdated. As a result, it lacked key functionality that others had added. For example, we were lacking complex option-trading capabilities and foreign exchange capabilities. Based upon various surveys, our existing clients were generally satisfied with our capabilities, but it was becoming increasingly difficult to acquire new, larger, and more sophisticated clients without some of the advanced capabilities that our competitors already possessed.

Trading commissions were headed down, likely to zero. This trend was clear, and while we did not know when it would occur, we did know that we were poorly positioned for that eventuality. When the industry had started forty years earlier, the average commission for a hundred-share lot might have been upwards of $200 or more. This had made trading largely inaccessible for the average consumer.

Prior to the advent of the internet, you would call your broker, and he or she would place your trade directly into their proprietary system. In many instances, the broker would call you with a "good" trading or investing idea and charge you an exorbitant commission for the pleasure. Men like Johnson, Schwab, Ricketts, Waterhouse, and Riney saw the opportunity to reduce the need for the intermediaries of the big "wire houses" by building a low-cost, straightforward way for the average American to access the markets. It was a massive hit.

With the internet in play, pricing was going lower. Scottrade had initially led the way, beginning the price war with a commission of seven dollars per trade. This was the lowest price in the industry for quite a long time. Rodger had decided to be the price leader, and it had worked.

Scottrade took off and expanded rapidly. The other large self-directed firms, including Fidelity, TD Ameritrade, and Charles Schwab initially decided not to match Scottrade's low price. This gave Scottrade a decided advantage for years. It was a market pricing disruption that eventually generated a new trend.

When the larger players began to lose market share to Scottrade because of our lower commission price, expansive and localized branch network, and a better value proposition, they began proactively negotiating pricing with their best customers when those customers threatened to leave. This trend was unsettling, and it caused average commission prices to go down further. Larger traders were now paying under the seven-dollar price point in many cases. Scottrade also had to begin negotiating to retain and grow clients. The price war grew more intense.

Another pricing trend was to give away free trades as part of new client acquisition marketing. This lowered commission prices again as clients hopped from broker to broker to receive, in some cases, dozens or even hundreds of free trades. Competitors also started offering outright cash for new accounts of a certain dollar amount. For example, a customer who deposited $10,000, might receive a $500 deposit from the company. These incentives were justified as a cost of acquisition and funded by the respective marketing budgets.

Some of these offers made no sense economically, but we had to play the game or find our clients leaving for another broker with a better offer. During this period, clients, especially the most active and most profitable ones, were in control. Profit margins were eroding, and competition for clients was fierce.

In April 2013, in the midst of this price war, the new fintech startup Robinhood came to market, offering zero commissions. Robinhood aggressively targeted the price-sensitive first-time investor. The company focused on providing access to the financial markets (or as they put it, "democratizing" investing) at a low cost of entry for new investors and traders.

Initially, Robinhood's technology was inferior and one-dimensional. Their offer was limited to a mobile application, and they did not offer mutual funds or other packaged products sometimes preferred by longer-term investors. They did not offer retirement accounts, which is a large percentage of all brokerage accounts. Still, Robinhood began to acquire large numbers of clients and built a powerful challenger brand. They could not be dismissed.

At Scottrade, and later at TD Ameritrade, we never lost large numbers of our best and most profitable clients to Robinhood. Occasionally one of our clients would threaten to move their business to Robinhood. We could usually convince them otherwise by explaining the deficiencies of Robinhood: no 24/7 client service, no desktop trading website, a very limited product suite, no retirement accounts, etc. But Robinhood was indeed putting pressure on industry pricing.

The inevitable slide to zero commissions for the rest of the industry seemed closer than ever.

The bank regulatory environment was becoming more intense. The company had launched Scottrade Bank a few years earlier in response to the demands of clients for a more integrated financial services experience in addition to our core trading and investing capabilities. This was an emerging trend. Our competitors, including Schwab, already had nationally chartered banks. And while Fidelity did not have a bank per se, they had built sophisticated cash management capabilities by tightly integrating a variety of third-party bank partners. Interestingly, UMB was one of Fidelity's very early bank partners and remains one today. Of course, the broker-dealers that were also banks were offering more integrated brokerage and banking services.

Starting a nationally chartered bank is no small task. After the 2008 financial crisis, banks came under intense scrutiny, especially from the primary national bank regulator, the Office of the Comptroller of the Currency (OCC). At Scottrade, we had some difficulty fully starting our newly formed bank and were working to get on the right side of regulators. This became a significant undertaking and a big distraction as we sought to improve our core trading capabilities and client experience. We hired dozens of risk, compliance, and oversight personnel to ensure that we were abiding by the bevy of rules and regulations. It was hard work. Eventually we were able to resolve regulator concerns.

Rodger had cancer, making his future uncertain. Rodger has two sons and a daughter. One son was working at Scottrade at the time, and the other son had done so previously; however, none of his children wanted to run the business if Rodger were unable to do so.

Despite his health condition, Rodger came to the office almost every day. An entrepreneur and a fierce competitor, Rodger loved the business, the people, and the challenges surrounding his work. He would often tell me to "do what we need to do to beat the competition." He did not like to lose.

With these issues on the table in the spring of 2015, Rodger began to wonder whether it was time to sell the company. I vividly remember the conversation in which he indicated to me that he was leaning strongly that way. From my perspective, his reasoning made perfect sense. The pressures had been building, the valuation was likely as high as it would ever be, and we were a valuable and scarce asset that one of our competitors would most certainly want to acquire. At that juncture, I had only been with the company for five months. The news was a gigantic hit to the gut.

Rodger Riney is among the most honorable, trustworthy, humble, values-driven leaders I have ever come across. Scottrade associates loved that Rodger walked around the office, visiting with them on a regular basis. He also held lunch meetings with associates at all levels and functions.

When Rodger traveled, he always found the nearest Scottrade branch office and visited with the associates. This practice sometimes resulted in challenges for me. Rodger would come back from these trips with issues and ideas for my team to tackle. Sometimes the issues were more anecdotes than problems, but Rodger insisted I investigate each one and report back with a resolution to the individual or team that raised the issue.

In this way, Rodger reminded me of Ned Johnson, and Crosby Kemper Jr. All three men came back from their interactions with front-line associates with new ideas to evaluate and issues to resolve. These interactions drove home two points. First, there is no detail too small; second, the best ideas often come from the associates who are closest to the customers.

Watching Rodger, I learned about the power of humility. One of the architects of an entire industry, Rodger habitually deflected praise onto others while diminishing his own contributions to the company, the industry, and the St. Louis community. I watched Rodger accept responsibility when things went wrong while putting others in the limelight when things went right. He gave millions of dollars to many causes in St. Louis, often quietly or anonymously, just for the satisfaction of making a difference.

Whatever decision Rodger made about selling the company, I assured him that I would be in his corner. This was my commitment, even though I had not even left my temporary apartment when Rodger first started contemplating the company's sale. "Here we go again," I said to Michelle. As always, she was incredibly supportive, but I could tell that this one truly bothered her. Once again, our future, including where we would be living, was uncertain.

One Friday afternoon, Rodger called me into his office to inform me that he had decided to put the company on the market. I could see that he was filled with emotion, uncertainty, disappointment, and probably some doubt surrounding the prospect of the sale. But Rodger knew, as did I, that it was the right time and right environment in which to test the waters.

Rodger asked me to work with Drew Dennison, our CFO and COO, to help put the pitch book together. Given that we were a private company with limited publicly-disclosed information, this would be a significant task. We would need to generate a fair chunk of the required information from scratch.

I pledged my support to Rodger, promising to do whatever was needed to get this done. I assured him that I would fulfill my commitment to Scottrade and my team, regardless of the circumstances. Knowing that the days and weeks ahead were going to be difficult, I geared up to do the best job possible and get Rodger the highest possible valuation. Not only was this the right thing to do, but I also genuinely wanted the best possible outcome for Rodger and his family.

We hired Goldman Sachs to assist us with the sale process. Rodger said from the outset that he was not necessarily going to sell the company to the highest bidder. He had other important considerations for an eventual buyer. While there were hundreds of considerations, the most important ones boiled down to these four.

Sell to a strategic buyer. Typically, strategic buyers are from the same industry and have an ability to capture synergies as a result of an acquisition. While many only think of cost synergies, there are, in fact, many other forms of synergies, including revenue, product, technology, marketing, cross-selling, and more. Strategic buyers are generally willing to pay a premium to acquire the asset since capturing post-deal closing revenue and expense synergies enables the company to pay more.

Financial buyers, on the other hand, typically are not from the same industry, may not possess the knowledge to capture synergies, and may not even have the expertise to effectively run the business. Many prospective financial buyers, including banks, insurance companies, mutual fund companies, credit card companies, and foreign entities were interested. Rodger concluded that none of those would be a good fit. He wanted a strong, reputable strategic buyer that could make the combined client and associate experience better than the one that Scottrade could offer on its own. That left many who wanted a shot at the company outside the process.

Ensure that the buyer would commit to retain a large portion of the Scottrade branch network. Rodger understood that the branch network would need to be trimmed to eliminate overlapping locations with the buyer, but he would not allow his network to be decimated. His convictions about the importance of face-to-face contact in local markets remained unshaken. With this condition, the buyer might need to carry more expense and might, as a consequence, pay less for the company. That was okay with Rodger. He wanted the client experience to be enhanced after the acquisition, not diminished.

Require the buyer to keep a significant workforce in St. Louis. While this condition might limit synergies and thereby reduce the price a buyer might be willing to pay, Rodger was adamant about this condition. He was extremely proud of what he had accomplished in his hometown. In addition to employing more than a thousand local associates, Scottrade was a significant civic and community leader. Rodger would not be the kind of seller to cash out and leave his loyal associates in the lurch. Some dislocation of the associates was inevitable; Rodger would fight hard for extra benefits for those that would be affected. To give the employees who would be displaced time to find a new job, we ultimately negotiated for a more generous severance as compared to the industry norm.

Consider only buyers with a strong history of performance. Given that stock was going to be part of the consideration, the buyer had to be a reputable firm that Rodger believed in. He was making a bet that the combined firm would perform well and that the stock price would eventually rise after the acquisition. It had to be a synergistic proposition.

In the end, although many firms came knocking, and many more firms wanted to make a bid, Rodger concluded that only three firms met his requirements.

It was now late August, and events were moving at a furious pace. We set the in-person prospective buyer meetings for the week of Labor Day. We would do three meetings back-to-back over three successive days. Each of the prospective acquiring firms' top leaders would travel to St. Louis for their meeting.

The Scottrade deal team consisted of Drew Dennison; Kim Wells, our head of marketing; Adym Rygmyr, our general counsel; Chris McComish, the president of Scottrade Bank; and me. Rodger chose not to be present for these meetings, insisting we could handle them and that he would not add much to the discussions. We all believed that we needed him there. In the end, he decided that he would come in and say hello each morning and then exit, leaving the meetings in our hands.

Upon reflection, I realized how difficult it would be for Rodger to participate in a discussion about the sale of his beloved Scottrade. While he knew, and we all knew, that to sell was likely the right business decision, one can only imagine how difficult it would be to sell something you spent your entire professional career building. It's not easy to hand over something that represents your life's work.

I was asked to lead the discussions and to provide the history and review the firm's current operations. Having been at the company for only seven months at that point, I was extremely nervous and thought someone else would be a better choice. Rodger told me more than once that he had confidence in my ability to fulfill this role.

In the days prior to the meetings, I worked hard to learn every fact and figure that I could about the company. I was also committed to learning the culture and the softer side of the company so I could convey the heart of Scottrade with confidence.

It seemed to me that the best way to do this was in the form of customer and associate experiences. I went to work and uncovered hundreds of positive client and associate stories. I used those stories to communicate the real essence and value of the company. In the final analysis, buyers pay for a firm's assets and its future growth prospects. While it is hard to put an exact price tag on a positive customer and associate culture, the value is undeniable.

At the end of each day, the deal team briefed Rodger on the day's discussions and gave him our individual and collective perspectives about the prospective buyer. By the end of the third day, all the members of the team were exhausted. It seemed like every conceivable question had been asked and answered from every possible angle.

At the conclusion of the third meeting, the Scottrade deal team sat down with Rodger and the team from Goldman Sachs to formally assess the three competing bids. At this point, we did not have firm final offers, only nonbinding indications of interest. Despite that, we determined quite easily that company number one was not a good fit, while company number two or company number three might be.

Not wanting to show our hand too early, we kept all three at the table negotiating and playing them against each other over the next few weeks. Next, we asked each bidder to prepare a final offer, including the total purchase price, the form of consideration (cash versus stock), and any other conditions they wanted to include with their bid. While that was happening, those of us on the deal team needed to keep the company running—and keep the needs of our associates and clients at the center of our decision making.

In addition to the strain of countless meetings, late nights, and weekends, I empathized with the associates. I found it difficult to look them in the eye each day as they went about their business. Scottrade was the only company many of them had ever worked for. I struggled, knowing that loyal employees would be negatively affected by an eventual deal, and I felt badly that they had no idea that anything was going on around them. Still, it would be much worse if rumors were flying around without the benefit of all the facts. We needed to make sure that associates heard about the sale from Rodger once the buyer agreed to the deal and its provisions. We would do our best to make as many of these provisions as possible in the best interest of our associates.

Finally, the offers were presented, and the evaluation process commenced. Because Rodger had a strong set of principles and conditions he wanted to see in the acquirer, the process was somewhat less difficult than might be imagined. Rodger was able to put each bidder's deal terms up against his set of objective criteria and make a judgment. In the final analysis, TD

Ameritrade was the perfect fit. The company was a strategic buyer that would benefit from the additional scale that Scottrade would bring. TD Ameritrade understood how to build strong client experiences and the value of face-to-face relationships in cementing those relationships.

The consideration was to be 75 percent cash and 25 percent stock. In terms of the branch network, the soft agreement was to consolidate about 150 locations. However, there was also an understanding that the best branch in a particular market would remain, so in some cases, a TD Ameritrade branch would be closed versus a Scottrade one.

TD Ameritrade was a highly reputable organization with a stellar brand and the backing of TD Bank, which is one of Canada's largest, strongest, and most reputable financial institutions. TD Ameritrade committed to keep a client services and operations presence in St. Louis. While there would be job losses across the branch system and St. Louis headquarters functions, Rodger had done all he could do to limit those losses. And by requiring additional consideration in the form of enhanced severance for affected associates, he felt comfortable that he had done the best that he could do for his company, his city, his associates, and his family.

While the prospective deal had largely been kept under wraps, leaks began to circulate on Friday, October 21, just two days before the board was scheduled to meet for the final sale approval. News that a deal was possibly in the works was all over CNBC and other media outlets, including the media serving St. Louis.

Several times in the past, rumors of a possible sale had surfaced. Each time, Rodger had immediately denied the rumors. This time he could not do so. This made for a challenging weekend as associates wondered whether this time the threat was real. I avoided the phone, emails, texts, and every other form of communication over the course of the weekend. We put our heads down until we could get the deal approved at Sunday's board meeting and announce it early Monday morning.

In many respects, the board meeting was anticlimactic; the deal terms had already been agreed upon and Rodger and his family had control of the company's voting shares. It was still a highly emotional moment as Rodger and his wife, Paula, who had joined us for the meeting, prepared for the gravity of the vote about to take place.

The sale would mean the end of an independent Scottrade and, over time, the loss of the Scottrade name. This was particularly poignant as the name of the arena in downtown St. Louis (where the St. Louis Blues played professional ice hockey) was named the Scottrade Center. TD Ameritrade had already made the decision not to assume the arena name. The loss of Scottrade would be another in a long succession of St. Louis headquartered companies that had either been sold or relocated out of state. We knew that the local community would take the news hard.

After reviewing the deal terms with the board and discussing it a final time, Rodger asked for the vote to approve the sale. The company would be sold for a little over $4 billion. It was a complicated transaction in that the Scottrade broker dealer and the registered investment advisor were sold to TD Ameritrade, while Scottrade Bank was sold to TD Bank. This tri-party transaction would make the upcoming integration planning even more difficult than ususal.

I found it hard to sleep that evening, and Monday morning came quickly. We assembled the company's leadership early in one of our large auditoriums, linking to our other sites by video. Given that the story had leaked at the end of the previous week, our focus was to confirm the story, review the details, and, most important, discuss the implications on our associates.

Rodger did a masterful job in his humble and unassuming way of explaining the deal rationale. Everyone knew of his illness and the other pressures taking place in the industry, so in some ways, the sale was not a complete shock. Still, it was a surprise and a personal grief for many.

Scottrade associates and many clients demonstrated a high commitment to the brand. In some ways it was like confirming the death of a loved one.

Announcements of this type take time for individuals to process. At first blush, people naturally ask, "What will happen to me, my career, and my family?" In our initial communication, we wanted to assure the associates that none of the forthcoming changes would happen quickly. No one would immediately be out of a job. It would take months, if not years, before the deal closed and the new owner began to shape the company.

Over the next few weeks, I had dozens of one-on-one and group meetings with worried associates. We needed to help associates understand what it meant for them while keeping everyone focused on serving our clients. After all, we had a company to run.

Given the unsettled nature of the months leading up to the sale, I wasn't focused on what the sale meant for me. I thought about it, but with the overwhelming workload and my concern for the associates, my personal concerns could wait. While I had been with Scottrade for less than a year at the time of the deal announcement, I was confident that I'd find something meaningful when my work was done there. I was not excited about the prospect of changing jobs and possibly moving again, but I'd face those challenges when the time came.

Despite my short tenure at Scottrade, I learned a lot about myself and leadership. Knowing Rodger and learning from him as a leader was a highlight. His humility and commitment to his associates, even in the face of tough business decisions, as I've already noted, was remarkable. The collaboration and self-sacrifice of the entire ELT for the sake of the business provided a model of leadership effectiveness for me. The same was true of the collaboration of the deal team. In both groups, there was the clear understanding that we worked for a greater good than our own departments, wallets, or recognition. These all contributed to the ongoing development of my mosaic.

Once again, I had found myself in a situation I could neither control nor influence, which was, at times, frustrating. I had no control, and limited influence, over Rodger's decision to sell the company. It was the right thing to do at the right time. Knowing that did not make it any easier to deal with. As we ran the company and headed toward closing the deal and integration over the next year, I had to constantly remind myself to focus on the things I could control. These included my attitude, focus, and commitment to do a great job regardless of the circumstances and how they might affect me, my career, and my family.

When TD Ameritrade CEO Tim Hockey asked me to join his executive team to lead the retail division, my next career step became clear. The long period of secrecy required between the time I accepted the job and the regulatory process needed to announce the leadership change was difficult on a number of levels. In the end, that scenario was one of a number of elements that affected my time with the company.

Chapter 9

Driving Positive Change in a Sea of Ambiguity: TD Ameritrade

TD Ameritrade was a technology-driven entrepreneurial organization created in 1975 from the vision and genius of Joe Ricketts. Joe grew up in Nebraska City, attended college in Omaha, and built his great American company largely from there. It hadn't been easy. There were missteps along the way, some of which damaged the business in the early days. Still, Joe focused on doing what was right for his customers and had the outsized idea to reimagine the brokerage business from his office on the American Plains. While it took some time, his hard work, along with his customer-centric and highly ethical approach, began to yield results. Once the internet became mainstream, Joe grabbed hold of the opportunity it afforded, and accelerated growth began.

My time at TD Ameritrade was influenced by a convergence of several elements. Some were controllable ones. Three significant ones were not. Their selecting me to head the retail division (and the secrecy that surrounded the selection) was the first element.

When the announcement was finally made that I would be replacing incumbent Tom Bradley, it was met with shock, confusion, and dismay, internally and externally. Articles in various publications questioned the wisdom of the move. One article in *RIABiz* was particularly noteworthy.

Here are some of the quotes from the article that caused me, and others, quite a bit of angst.

> Matthew Cooper, president of Beacon Pointe Advisors: "It's a stunning move. I was definitely surprised by it and didn't expect it. When you compare the two brands, Scottrade and TD, I'd expect that all of the senior leadership at TD would remain."

> TD spokesman Joseph Giannone: "de Silva is stronger than Bradley culturally, technically and functionally, which made it 'logical' to decide on him over Bradley. The magnitude of this integration presents some unique needs, both cultural and technical. We believe Peter has functional experience and can help provide a strong cultural fit. Asking someone like him to join our executive leadership team was a strong logical decision."

> Cecile Munoz, founder, U.S. Executive Search & Consulting: "If the decision were made through the lens of supporting and expanding a thriving culture through integration and beyond, then we must assume they asked the right questions to get to the right answers. One thing is certain, the industry will be closely watching TD's new retail chief."

> Wealth management analyst Alois Pirker: "Bradley is proven. I don't think de Silva was at Scottrade very long. Having been chosen that pairing against Bradley, he better be very good. No doubt he will be."

What an introduction to a new role at a new company!

The second element was the unexpected and untimely departure of CEO Tim Hockey a year and a half later. The third element was the highly volatile and competitive marketplace during that period. Navigating my way required patience and persistence. At the same time, this period enabled me to better understand and solidify many of my leadership principles.

This role helped me forge a deeper understanding of and appreciation for the principles that endure across diverse leaders, industries, and situations.

My first few weeks following the official change in leadership were highly stressful. I needed to learn the TD Ameritrade organization; build a leadership team; successfully establish a process to steer a massive client conversion; build trust with my new TD Ameritrade team and colleagues; reassure the 5,000-plus TD Ameritrade and Scottrade retail associates that things were going to be okay; and quickly build credibility within the organization's hierarchy.

I also needed to build a strong and trusting relationship with my new boss, Tim Hockey. I felt a lot of pressure to perform for Tim since he was the one who selected me over a popular and long-tenured incumbent. I resolved not to let Tim down, no matter what.

Tim was clear up front about the expectations he had of me and all his leaders. Shortly after I joined his team, he sent me his "User's Manual to Tim Hockey." I had been advised by other team members that this was coming, so it was not a big surprise when it arrived in my email inbox. The document comprised a combination of Tim's background and history, personal and performance expectations, values, and belief systems. This was a different way for a leader to introduce himself to a new direct report, but I found it helpful in terms of starting our relationship on the right foot.

One section of the manual, titled "What I'm Like," set expectations for working for Tim. It included items such as "I am very loyal," "I'm an early morning guy," and "I don't take myself too seriously."

Another section was titled "What I Believe and How I Try to Act and Lead." In this section Tim explains: "I don't 'work' 24/7, but I'm 'on' 24/7; there's a difference." Another of his expectations reads, "Be honest and be early." I particularly liked this statement: "I believe that organizations should have a 'No Jerks' policy." Amen to that.

When I joined the organization, TD Ameritrade was essentially involved in three businesses:

1) institutional/registered investment advisor custody, which was a business-to-business (B2B) channel; 2) direct retail, which was a business-to-consumer (B2C) channel; and 3) active trader, which was small in terms of client numbers but large in terms of activity and revenue contribution. This segment worked hand in glove with the retail business segment, my specific area of responsibility. Tim ran the three businesses in a semiautonomous manner, seeking to leverage synergies where they existed.

Minimal points of leverage existed between the retail and institutional businesses. My colleague, Tom Nally, was a capable, well-liked leader and we got along very well. We collaborated where it made sense, such as when clients migrated between the institutional and retail platforms, on shared infrastructure and collaborating with TD Bank, but we did not seek leverage that was not there. Tim respected and supported our approach.

On the active trader side of the business, Steve Quirk or "Q," had come to TD Ameritrade through the acquisition of the then industry-leading thinkorswim active trader platform a few years prior. Q was a highly respected leader in the trader sphere and a genuinely good guy.

Q held responsibility for active trader product development and the client segment. While the number of active trader clients was small compared to the total number of retail clients, these clients traded at a disproportionately high rate, thus driving significant trading volume, margin lending, revenues, and profitability. I led all the other retail client segments: products, digital, services, sales, investment management, and client experience.

Obvious opportunities for greater collaboration existed between the retail and trader teams. One opportunity concerned the way the branch associates spent their time. Retail branch associates were instructed not to proactively engage with active trader clients, who were the sole clients of the trader phone-based team. This made little sense to me. From my perspective, all TD Ameritrade clients should be served by all channels (phone, branch, and digital).

A conversation with Q provided the history. In the past, a few branch associates had called on active trader clients to sell them investment products.

The clients complained to their active trader teams, saying that they did not want to be sold investment products, nor did they want a branch representative to contact them. After a few of these incidents, rules of engagement were established, prohibiting branch associates from proactively engaging with active trader clients. While I respected this concern, I thought there had to be a mutually beneficial way to approach these critically important clients and provide them with an even better total TD Ameritrade experience.

Some leaders had allowed a few unfortunate incidents to drive policy and procedure changes that were not necessarily good for the active trader client base or the business. It was an example of policy by anecdote. We were looking at our clients as having monoline needs when they had a wide variety of needs, most of which we could serve. I remember coming up with the phrase "Traders invest, and investors trade," meaning that we shouldn't completely segment clients. Clients have multiple unmet needs (some primary, some secondary) that the company should seek to fulfill. I mentioned this idea at a staff meeting. Tim immediately liked it, and it became a rallying cry of sorts.

Research validated that our active trader clients did, indeed, invest—only not with us. They were investing elsewhere, either because they did not know the totality of our capabilities or, more important, no one was asking them about their overarching needs and goals. We had much less wallet share with our clients than we might, in part because we were not addressing the full scope of their needs. Q recognized this as well, but he was hesitant to open the active trader clients up for discussions with our branch planning associates. Misaligned incentives also played a role. Despite the challenges, Q and I made some good progress collaborating.

We developed a lead program across the branches and the active trader team. When an active trader lead was uncovered at a branch, the branch associate transferred that lead to a more experienced trading representative for a deeper dive. The branch associate was rewarded for that that action. The leads began to flow, and the program was quite successful. This is a good example of success in aligning organizations and incentives. As at

UMB and Scottrade before TD Ameritrade, its associates, and its clients benefited from a more focused "One TD Ameritrade" approach.

Still, this organizational structure created missed opportunities. Over time, I had numerous conversations with Tim about it. My direct reports were often frustrated by the lack of cohesiveness across the lines of business, resulting in an under-optimization of product, technology, and service priorities. Our internal business partners were also asking for a more holistic approach to prioritizing.

Tim understood my point and even expressed some of his own frustration with the structure as it was, but he made it clear that this was the way he wanted to run the organization. Because the trader segment was a critical revenue, earnings, and growth driver, Tim felt it was important to keep it a separate entity, one reporting directly to him. I think it also had something to do with the fact that the trader segment was an acquired part of the business and agreements I wasn't privy to were established at the time of the acquisition.

I pride myself on being flexible and adaptable to new environments and approaches. I had overcome organizational ambiguity at Fidelity, UMB, and Scottrade, thriving despite it. I had come to appreciate that there is no such thing as a perfect organizational structure.

By the time I started at TD Ameritrade, I had formulated the principle "Align strategy, structure, and people"—in that order. With responsibility for one of the three businesses under Tim, I didn't have control of the company. I could work toward alignment in my own division.

It was imperative that I develop deep and trusting relationships with my leadership peers, especially with Q, Tom Nally, and Denise Karkos, our chief marketing executive.

Well respected inside the company and the industry, Tom was a longtime TD Ameritrade leader. He ran the fast-growing institutional business successfully. Denise was an award-winning marketing executive and leader.

She had been responsible for some excellent branding work and was in the process of modernizing our marketing efforts. The majority of work Denise undertook and most of the marketing budget was on behalf of the retail customer and brand. This necessitated a tight relationship between Denise's teams and mine.

Although I got along well with each of these individuals, there was tension, and I sometimes struggled to work with them as a group. Some of the tension had to do with organizational ambiguity. Sometimes, it was hard to tell who was responsible for what or what the priorities were. Other factors, including the fact that my appointment to the job over Tom Bradley was kept secret for months, may have influenced the relationships as well.

Tim noticed the tension building. In response, he asked me, the new team member, to complete a 360-degree review. This review is a diagnostic, multidimensional feedback process in which an individual receives aggregated information from his or her boss, peers, subordinates, and other business partners. The individual then participates in debriefing the feedback, typically with each person or group that participated in the review.

I had completed 360-degree reviews numerous times in the past and always found them useful in developing strategies to work better, primarily with my peers and across each of the constituencies. I was frustrated that Tim hadn't asked the entire leadership team to take the survey simultaneously, which is more typical. With that approach, different team member styles are assessed, and individuals and teams develop strategies to work better together.

The report I received about a month later confirmed some of what I expected. I was perceived as a strong leader who set excellent direction. I was strategic and focused on improving performance. I held people accountable and drove for results. Everyone, including Tim, gave me strong marks around all the quantitative measures of getting things done. My direct reports gave me high marks for supporting them, building effective teams, communicating, and being committed to their personal and professional development.

The areas for improvement were around collaboration, primarily with my peer group. The respondents suggested I could do a better job of being a team player and putting the group's success above my own. This feedback was particularly concerning to me; I had always thought I did a good job in this regard. Some feedback from colleagues indicated that I was too aggressive regarding change and might consider throttling it down a little. My colleagues also suggested that I stay in my own swim lane and focus on those things I was directly responsible for. In other words, they felt I was interfering in areas that were not my business.

Given that I've always considered myself a strong collaborator and had not heard this specific feedback before, I was troubled. I wondered how much of the feedback was related to my intrinsic style and how much was related to the ambiguous situation that I found myself in. In the end it did not matter. I was not going to make excuses. I needed to adjust my behavior and improve my relationships with my peers.

Shortly after receiving the survey results, internalizing them, and building an action plan, I met with Tim. Before the meeting, I decided that I was going to do something I had rarely done before. I told him the entire story of my lifelong struggle with CMT. I felt this background might provide better context for him as we worked together. You can imagine how nervous I was about taking this step. I trusted Tim, but I still had no idea how he would react. My worst-case scenario was that he would think I might not be up to the job. Surprisingly, nothing awful happened.

Tim listened carefully and immediately offered his unqualified support. He asked questions about the nature of CMT, seeking to understand. He in no way treated me with pity or implied that he thought less of me. He did not offer any accommodations, nor was I looking for any (as none were necessary).

Tim encouraged me to tell the others on his leadership team and my direct reports about my condition. I didn't want to, but I eventually decided to follow Tim's advice. I concluded that complete transparency was the best way to go. Transparency would help others better understand me, which might lead to stronger relationships.

This was a big step. My internal resistance was still strong. I heard my parents emphasizing that my health was no one's business but my own. Seemingly, that perspective had served me well up to this point. It was time to change.

What would my colleagues think of me if they knew I was fighting with pain every day? How would they treat me? My positive experience with Tim gave me some comfort as I thought about telling my peers, but I was still nervous. This was a big behavioral shift for me.

Four Recommendations for Building Trust

Researchers Kimberly Nei and Darin Nei studied data across thirty independent studies to examine the relationship between personality and ethical leadership. They wanted to know what leaders should do to build trust with new teams.

They published their findings in a 2018 *Harvard Business Review* article called "Don't Try to Be the 'Fun Boss' — and Other Lessons in Ethical Leadership." Here is a summary of their recommendations.

1. **Be humble, not charismatic.** While charisma can help you command attention and engage others in your organizational mission, too much charisma can get you in trouble. The authors claim that too much charisma will lead to a reputation of self-absorption and self-promotion. "The team may start to worry that you will no longer do what is best for the team or organization, and that you will instead do what is best for your own agenda."

2. **Be steady and dependable.** For your team members to trust you, they need to be confident you will remain true to your words and deliver on your promises, all for the good of the organization.

> Exercise good judgment, take calculated risks, and adhere to organizational principles.
>
> 3. **Remember that modesty is the best policy.** Although it can be nice to be the boss who is informal and lighthearted, people expect a degree of responsibility and professionalism from the boss. Keeping some distance between you and your team sends signals that you "are there for their professional benefit and that they can rely on you when needed."
>
> 4. **Be vigilant.** Typically, the first few months in a new leadership role is a time of observing, learning, and adjusting. During that time, leaders are mindful of and intentional about the impressions they are making on others. As they become more comfortable in their roles, they pay less attention to these things. The leader's "dark-side tendencies" can emerge and interfere with success. Successful leaders stay vigilant and seek feedback on an ongoing basis.
>
> Nei and Nei remind us that the personality characteristics that lead to our promotions to leadership positions are not always the ones that lead to success in the new role. They maintain that "spending too much time trying to get noticed or having a 'win at all costs' mentality to get ahead can put you (and your team) at a higher risk of engaging in unethical behavior. Having awareness of your surroundings and an understanding of the ways you influence your team will help to keep yourself (and your team) on track."

Over the next few weeks, I had individual conversations with each member of Tim's leadership team. I took a deep breath before each conversation, thanked each person for his or her feedback, and pledged to improve in the suggested areas. Then I said that there was something else I wanted to talk about. I described my CMT and how it likely shaped me into the person I was. I explained how the ridicule I experienced as a child motivated me to keep my health challenges private to protect myself from more ridicule. I explained how difficult this conversation was for me. I expressed my hope that they would not look at me any differently. In the spirit of trust and transparency, it was time for them to know.

The response was genuinely gracious and supportive. I should not have been overwhelmed, but I was. A few weeks later, I sat down with my own leadership team and had the same discussion, with the same result. This was a watershed moment for me.

During those conversations, I was also able to share my perspectives about our collective work and discuss ways we could work together more productively. Openness and trust began to emerge in these relationships. Despite my initial objections, these were satisfying and productive conversations that helped to break through some barriers.

My expectations and my colleagues' reactions to the disclosure of my CMT condition were miles apart. This should have caused me step back and consider my lifelong stance of keeping my CMT a secret. I can't say that it did, at least not at that time. Looking back, I don't think I was quite ready to fully open up.

Without ever thinking it through, I equated vulnerability with weakness. I always had. Consequently, I noticed the difference between the response I expected from my colleagues and the one I received, but I held that observation at a distance. I couldn't afford to appear weak. Still, this experience cracked open the door for a shift of a longstanding, even rigid, section in my personal and leadership mosaic. Another experience opened the door even further.

The spring before the sale of TD Ameritrade, Tim took his entire leadership team on a three-day offsite session at West Point, the US military academy in New York. Upon arrival, I discovered that the experience would include participation on an obstacle course. My heart sank.

Although I had already disclosed my CMT to my peers, I was profoundly frightened to display any physical limitations. Distracted, I lived in dread until rain caused the program leaders to announce that we wouldn't be able to go outside. We would do some stretching and a few other exercises indoors, but not the full course.

Just as I was starting to relax, the weather cleared. We would go outside after all. Now we had to do the whole obstacle course in the cold and mud. The situation was worse than ever. I remember someone remarking, "Peter, you don't have to do this," but I've never been one to take an easy out.

The larger group was broken into teams in which members were instructed to work together. Success would be defined by the entire team completing the course. Individual performance and time to completion wouldn't matter, and we weren't competing against the other team. We were to work together to ensure that every individual made it to the end of the course. Still, I expected to drag the group's performance down and felt badly about it. I would do my best and somehow power through, but I knew it wasn't going to be pretty.

I'm not sure what I was expecting, but it wasn't what happened. One colleague said to me, "Peter, we are going to get you over the damn wall whatever it takes. We will work together to get everyone to the finish line." Each of us supported the other and even had a good laugh along the way. There was a sense of elation in overcoming the obstacles together. This was a bonding experience, just as it was intended to be. For me it was a unique and profoundly moving experience.

Had I not been open about my CMT with my peers, the obstacle course would have turned out differently. I would have muddled through, but I would have been embarrassed. The existing barriers between me and my colleagues, at least from my point of view, would have grown rather than diminished.

As a result of this episode, I became just a little bit more open to the idea that exposing vulnerability isn't the worst thing in the world. Maybe vulnerability didn't have to equal weakness and shame. Maybe vulnerability had a productive place in leadership after all. I can't say I knew what that productive place might be, but the door in my mosaic opened further, which was a healthy thing. A jagged shard was starting to shine.

I worked under the structure that Tim chose for the organization. After a few months of observation and extensive conversations with other senior leaders inside and outside my direct line of responsibility, I was ready to announce changes to my team's structure and leadership.

As you know, I believe that strategy should drive structure. Choosing the people to support the strategy and structure logically comes last. While we did not have the long-term strategy completely figured out, I knew enough about where I thought we needed to go to make near-term changes. I also knew that the most important thing we needed to accomplish in the near term was to successfully execute the Scottrade conversion. I needed to make sure that any structural changes helped us meet that mission-critical objective. The structure might need to change again as the strategy came into sharper focus, and that was okay. Also, I understood the types of leaders I would need along with their leadership skills and characteristics.

Most new leaders are faced with this conundrum of when to reorganize after starting in a new role. It is almost expected that leaders will make some changes quickly to begin to shape the organization in their image. How many times have you heard that the new leader is going to take ninety days to understand the organization before making any big changes, or that she is going to go on a listening tour to observe and learn first-hand what changes might be appropriate? The essential point at this early stage is to avoid doing harm by acting prematurely.

After my ninety-day period, it was obvious to me that I did not have all the talent I would need in every position as we moved ahead. I needed leaders who were strategic, bold, innovative, respected across the organization, and strong communicators. I also wanted leaders who were informed by the past but not beholden to it. I have an old saying that "there is no future in the past." I always tell my leaders to look out the front windshield, not the rear-view mirror.

The leaders who needed to move on were each fine and capable individuals. They had brought us to the current level of success, and I respected each one of them. Unfortunately, these leaders did not possess the combination of skills, abilities, or cultural sensitivities to remain part of the new team. I have always been committed to treating individuals at any level with respect and dignity, especially when making and executing difficult people-related decisions. Accordingly, I met with each person individually as part of the organizational change effort.

There's a terrific book written by Marshall Goldsmith called *What Got You Here Won't Get You There*. In it, Goldsmith describes how nuances can make the difference for successful people to become even more successful. I have found his teachings helpful. In fact, I have given his book to many individuals experiencing key life and career transitions.

I flew to Los Angeles on a Sunday to meet with the first person affected by the decision early on a Monday morning. Then it was off to Omaha to meet with the second person. The third person resided in Jersey City. As that individual worked for someone who reported to me, that leader had the initial discussion. I followed up by flying to Jersey City to meet with this individual's team. The entire process was emotional and draining. While people and organizational design changes were expected, the changes I implemented were beyond what many were expecting. It was now clear to everyone that I was, in fact, leading the retail organization.

While the retail teams from Scottrade and TD Ameritrade were getting better acquainted and integrated, there was still the massive issue of the Scottrade client conversion to work through. We were preparing to migrate three million Scottrade client accounts and over $200 billion in client assets to the TD Ameritrade platform. This was one of the largest industry client conversions of the decade—with no margin for error. If the conversion did not go flawlessly, we would lose clients and thus the value of the acquisition. It had to go perfectly.

There were dozens of work streams and thousands of decisions to make and items to address before we could convert the clients to the TD Ameritrade platform. Fortunately, James Kostulias, our conversion team leader, had been involved in many prior successful conversions. My confidence in him and the broader team was high. James was a direct report of mine after a recent organizational transition, so ultimate accountability was with me for a successful conversion event. A lot was resting on my shoulders.

Following the deal closing in September of 2017, the conversion team worked together to solve many critical items and make the necessary tradeoffs. Our long list of concerns included client experience, technology integration, branch footprints, marketing, branding, cost, and associate experience. Here are some of critical issues we faced in these areas.

Client Experience. Paramount among the conversion success measurements was to complete a seamless and smooth client experience. Each of our decisions had the potential to negatively affect the conversion and the post-conversion Scottrade client experience. For example, if we made Scottrade clients change account numbers and login instructions, a high probability existed that clients would not have this information handy come conversion day. To prevent this, we required the technology team to build a reference table so clients could keep their current Scottrade credentials.

We also terminated some Scottrade features, including the popular Scottrade Flexible Reinvestment Program (affectionately called FRIP). This feature was an early harbinger of fractional shares investing, something that would become popular across the industry over the next few years. We knew this decision would result in some client dissatisfaction, but it would be cost- and time-prohibitive to build the capability as part of the conversion effort. We were balancing time, cost, and client experience. We knew we needed to focus and finish.

Technology. We knew from the start that it was neither desirable nor possible to replicate the Scottrade client experience on the TD Ameritrade platform. In fact, our deal synergies assumed a complete migration of Scottrade clients to the then-current TD Ameritrade platform, with the Scottrade platform being 100 percent decommissioned. Although the amount of development on the TD Ameritrade platform would be negligible, we still needed to build a way to convert clients to the new platform without disruption. It took nearly a year to get the conversion code written, tested, and ready for execution.

Branch Footprints. Among the most difficult and emotional parts of the conversion effort was determining how best to combine the two branch footprints. Scottrade had nearly five hundred branches while TD Ameritrade had closer to 125. Like McDonald's and Burger King, or CVS and Walgreens, branches were, in many cases, right across the street from each other. In some instances, the locations were in the same shopping plaza, with shared parking.

Working through the physical branch office strategy and accounting for the people associated with those offices was highly complex. While there had been an informal agreement to keep the preponderance of the Scottrade branch network, that exact number was not expressly defined in the sale agreement.

Both teams were committed to maintaining a large and vibrant branch network, but the leaders had somewhat different perspectives on what the final combined number should be. TD Ameritrade was more of a technology-focused company; Scottrade was born of a strong commitment to service, particularly face-to-face service. The teams had a difficult time coming up with and agreeing upon a final and acceptable configuration. In the end it would be up to me to make a recommendation to Rodger and Tim.

I was under a ton of pressure on this one. On the one hand, I had Rodger telling me that we should keep the maximum number of branches open to retain clients and maintain the Scottrade client experience. On the other hand, Tim and the TD Ameritrade team were encouraging me to close or consolidate as many branch offices as possible to accelerate savings and rapidly transition more service activities to the internet.

We had a third-party consultant help us develop a series of options ranging from closing just a few branches to closing more than 250, which would have represented almost half of the Scottrade network. After much discussion, debate, and disagreement, I ultimately recommended to Tim and Rodger that we consolidate approximately 150 overlapping locations, bringing the combined network close to 350. This was still much larger than Schwab, Fidelity or E*TRADE had at the time. This number of closed branches was more than Rodger had wanted and less than Tim and the TD Ameritrade team wanted. Neither side was entirely happy with the outcome, but both could live with it, so it must have been a reasonable compromise.

Marketing and Branding. In an acquisition like this, two key questions arise: What will happen to the acquired company's brand? How much marketing muscle will the brand receive during the period from transaction close through client conversion? The answers are not always as complicated as they at first seem. Our acquisition announcement was made in October 2016, but we did not close the deal until September 2017, nearly a year later. Given that we were still independent organizations during that period, we needed and, in fact, were required by federal law to continue to compete head-on and seek competitive advantages against each other. This makes sense given that any deal can unravel prior to closing. Thus, we continued to make modest investments in Scottrade client acquisition and brand marketing to grow the business.

Costs. We decided that we were going to be aggressive with respect to the conversion timeline. We wanted to limit the amount of time we needed to run two parallel platforms, brands, and organizations. We were fortunate to be able to complete some early conversion planning work while we were waiting for regulatory approvals. For each month the conversion was delayed, it cost the organization millions of dollars to keep both platforms and organizations running. We set a goal to capture the maximum number of synergies as quickly as possible.

Associate Experience. The most difficult part of any merger involves the people and respective corporate cultures. This was inevitably difficult because there was no way to avoid significant job loss in this merger. We had promised Wall Street there would be significant financial synergies by combining the two organizations. Most of those synergies would be in the form of compensation savings. That meant that people were going to lose their jobs. Tim had made a point of letting both teams know that the job losses would not occur solely at Scottrade; they would occur at TD Ameritrade as well. This created even more concern and consternation. We now had anxious associates in both companies. As things unfolded, we needed to ease fears as realistically as possible while building a positive associate experience for those who would remain with us. Fortunately, as part of the deal, we had negotiated a good severance package for those losing their jobs. Rodger was insistent on that.

One of my fundamental principles is to take care of the associates. They will take care of the clients, and the rest will take care of itself. I have seen this approach succeed throughout my entire professional career. Wherever I go, one of my first questions is about the health and vitality of the associate population. I ask to see associate survey data, seeking to identify opportunities to drive engagement higher. TD Ameritrade and Scottrade were associate-centered organizations with regular surveys of associate sentiments. Both had good overall associate sentiment.

We attempted to make the personnel component of the transition as fair as possible by adopting a strategy we labeled "Talent Wins." Tim felt strongly about this approach. We would assess like talent across the two organizations and then choose the best talent for each position for the go-forward team.

Talent Wins was an attempt to be as objective as possible when determining who would be part of the future consolidated team. It necessitated a good understanding of the performance of the Scottrade and the TD Ameritrade associates so an objective comparison could be made. It sounded like the perfect way to treat all associates fairly. However, Talent Wins quickly turned into an impossible situation to convey and manage. In fact, it ended up causing quite a bit of strife with the associate populations.

I vividly remember standing in front of a large group of Scottrade associates in St. Louis, attempting to explain the Talent Wins approach. At first, the associates responded positively. The idea seemed to make sense: compare talent across the two organizations and pick the best. Easy, right?

As the associates processed this idea, however, difficult questions arose:

- ✦ How would we compare an individual's performance across roles when the roles and job expectations were not the same?
- ✦ How would we address differences in success measurements, such as sales and client service targets?
- ✦ How would different leadership expectations and styles factor in?
- ✦ How would we compare performance when the products, technology, brands, and client bases were all different?
- ✦ How would the size of a branch office and the number of assigned clients be considered when evaluating individual and branch performance?
- ✦ How would we keep personal and organizational bias out of the assessment process?

Standing there in front of hundreds of associates, realizing I did not have good answers to these reasonable questions, it began to feel like we might have just snatched defeat from the jaws of victory. What had seemed like a good idea had not, in fact, been thoroughly considered. It was back to the drawing board.

In the end, we adopted a hybrid version of the Talent Wins approach whereby individuals were assessed based upon hard performance metrics, cultural fit, and an understanding as to how their skills would benefit the combined organization. The process was not perfect, but when we ultimately announced the realignments and reductions, most thought that we had done a reasonable job. When making organizational and personnel changes, the best you can hope for is that associates will understand how and why you came up with the decisions you did, even if they do not agree with them. I think we met that standard in this case.

The next few months were a flurry of activity as we continued to prepare for the Scottrade client conversion. A few weeks before D-Day, we were confident enough in our readiness to launch the all-important client communications work stream. As with any large conversion, we planned to complete this one over a weekend, giving us the time to revert in case anything major went wrong. We didn't really have a viable plan B. Plan A had to work.

One of the last things to complete prior to the conversion was to balance the conversion files. The purpose of this was to ensure that the appropriate number of shares, dollars, assets, and client accounts would be transferred from the Scottrade platform to the TD Ameritrade platform. We held our breath until Judy, the leader of our operations team, reported that the conversion files had balanced to the penny and to the share. A cheer went up when Judy announced the results. This was unheard of. All our hard work was paying off. After more than a year of planning, coding, testing, and retesting, we were ready to go.

Despite beliefs to the contrary, there is no magic lever to pull when you say, "Let's do it." A conversion is a lot less exciting than that. In essence, you inform the technology team to go ahead and run the next set of jobs and routines, which will transfer the data to the new platform. Once that is complete and another set of validations is performed, it is time to introduce clients to their new accounts and data.

I wanted to be the first person to see my accounts and data after the conversion. I remember sitting in the command center in St. Louis when word came that the data was now available for viewing. I was so nervous that the first time I tried to log in, I entered the wrong credentials and was prevented from seeing my new TD Ameritrade account. Fortunately, I got the login information right the second time. There was my account. Everything was perfect, just as it was supposed to be. Pride swept over me and the entire team as we realized that we had done it. The technology conversion was a success.

A tremendous amount of work was still ahead as we continued to learn how best to serve the former Scottrade clients in the new TD Ameritrade environment. Inbound client volumes ran at extremely high levels for the next few months as clients adjusted to the new platform. Despite our best planning, the onslaught of conversion-related volume, coupled with a positive stock market, put tremendous pressure on the service teams and our service performance suffered as a result. It took multiple tries over the next months to get our service levels back in line with our internal performance expectations.

A few months post-conversion, we asked Pricewaterhouse Coopers to conduct an after-conversion study to determine what we did right and what we might have done better. Their conclusion was that the conversion was an extremely well-planned and well-executed event. They went so far as to indicate that our conversion process was the new standard for large-scale financial services client conversions. The report noted as important keys to our success our intense focus on the client experience; assembling a strong, focused, accountable, and dedicated team; incentives that aligned with the outcome; and our ability to make tough decisions quickly. This was additional external proof that the team had done a terrific job.

I have been fortunate to have been part of conceiving, writing, and helping to execute multiple successful strategic plans throughout my career. Fidelity migrated from closed architecture to open architecture, from a mutual fund company to a brokerage company, and from customer service to client experience. These were key strategic thrusts that enabled the company to enjoy success over the decades.

At UMB, Mariner and I rewrote the playbook by focusing the company on more stable fee income generation through strategic investments in health savings accounts administration, wealth management, investment management, investment management services, and corporate trust services. These strategic shifts led to more predictable, higher-growth revenue and earnings, while maintaining a low credit risk profile. Wall Street rewarded the company with a price-to-earnings (P/E) ratio that was almost twice that of our traditional midsize bank peer group.

At Scottrade, we refocused the strategy to modernize our technology platform, enhance the product lineup to include managed investments, materially enhance the client experience, and better leverage our internal banking capabilities. While there was not enough time to see the fruits of this new strategic direction before the company's sale, I am confident we were on the right track.

While TD Ameritrade was performing well, growth in the retail segment had been slowing. Tim concluded that the entire company could benefit from an objective third-party review of the competitive environment, our current positioning within it, gaps in our current product and service offerings, and thoughts on the path forward. The senior operating committee (SOC), with input from a third-party consultant, began an intensive effort to create a refreshed purpose, mission, and strategic plan with the goal of accelerating business momentum. We spent countless hours debating the path forward.

At one of these strategy discussions, Tim remarked that there are fundamentally only three ways to successfully compete as an organization: product, price, or client experience. He maintained that strategy was about making hard choices. Failure to make hard choices will cause an organization to drift from one good idea to the next without a singular focus.

At first, I thought Tim's approach was too simplistic. Are there only three critical variables in strategy setting? After considering the question for some time, however, I came to appreciate that these actually were the three most important strategic variables an organization needs to consider. These three variables are not cumulative: You must pick one.

Apple, for example, has staked out its claim on product excellence; Walmart has staked out a claim on low prices; and Disney has a lock on client experience. This does not mean that these companies do not compete on some facets of all three variables. They do. But they made a conscious choice to distinguish themselves through just one of them in pursuit of a durable competitive advantage. Trying to be all things to all people is a surefire way to be nothing to nobody.

TD Ameritrade did some things extraordinarily well. We had the finest retail active-trader platform in the business. Our institutional platform had superior technology and an open architecture approach that distinguished it positively from its primary competitors, and our retail product, technology, and client experience were competitive. While these were excellent foundational elements, our growth was still slower than we knew it could be.

The SOC eventually decided that client experience would be our distinguishing characteristic. It would be our North Star. This would be the case for the entire TD Ameritrade enterprise, not only for retail. The focus on client experience became our rallying cry. Everything we did from then on focused on improving in that area.

At one strategy meeting, the SOC was discussing how to optimize the intersection more effectively between technology and our client-facing associates. Tim suggested that we consider creating a "high-tech, high-touch" client experience. I considered his statement for a few minutes and then offered a slightly different take on his theme.

I suggested instead that we build a "high-tech, *right*-touch" client experience. In this approach, we would always lead with technology, which was consistent with our market positioning, and we would complement that with the *right* touch. That touch could take the form of a phone call, email, text, a branch consultation, or whatever was right for the client's particular situation. The team liked it, and the phrase became a strategic theme as we progressed.

The refreshed strategic plan forced us to make hard choices rather than trying to be all things to all people. Our associates helped us create our new purpose statement: to transform lives and investing—for the better.

We resolved to segment our clients more precisely so that we could better target products, services, and marketing to more discrete client groups. An important element was to align customer experiences against segment and client revenues and profitability.

We needed to invest in creating better experiences for the clients who were the most profitable. We also needed to uncover more ways to enhance the relationship with TD Bank to benefit our clients. Each of these changes was focused on enhancing the client experience and improving profitability and returns to all stakeholders. Once we had a board-approved enterprise plan, the teams were focused on execution. This was an excellent example of embracing my principle, focus and finish.

As I've seen in other cases throughout my career, having a well-defined, well-articulated strategy is liberating. There is an old saying that if you don't know where you are going, then any path will get you there. Don't fall into that trap. Spend the time and energy to create clarity for all your internal and external stakeholders. From marketing and branding to operations and technology, priorities and nonnegotiables become clear once you have a strategy. Ladder your initiatives against your strategy. If they don't fit, dispense with them. Focus on what matters. Your associates will appreciate the strategic clarity and gain an understanding regarding how their efforts align with the bigger picture.

Tim formed a cross-enterprise strategic planning team to oversee the myriad of strategic initiatives. We were making steady progress on these initiatives when a shock occurred: No one expected the announcement following the July 2019 board meeting that Tim would be departing TD Ameritrade. When Tim assembled his leadership team to let us know, we sat in stunned silence. None of us knew what to make of this development. Tim had been in the role for two years and was a highly regarded, contemporary leader. He had been groomed at TD Bank, and by all accounts he seemed to have support from TD Bank leadership. No one inside or outside the firm had any inkling this was coming.

The abrupt and unexpected shift created a wave of anxiety across the organization. The next few weeks were challenging as the SOC sought to reassure associates and clients that the company's future was still on solid footing, which it was. My own leadership team resolved to stay focused and on the path we had established, unless we received new direction.

The executive search firm Spencer Stuart was retained to conduct an internal and external search for the new CEO. I asked Tim for his thoughts on whether the board would consider me as a viable candidate. He encouraged me to put my hat in the ring. After talking it through with Michelle, I decided to do so.

The period between Tim's announcement in July and late November, when the second shoe dropped, was an extremely challenging time. With Tim as a lame duck leader, it became increasingly difficult for him to make critical longer-term decisions. Rightfully, he did not want to tie the hands of his successor.

Here was another situation in which I had to put my head down and focus on the things I could control, while trying to influence those things that I thought were important. There were also some things that would need to wait until we had a new CEO, including decisions about how to better manage unprofitable clients, additional investments in digitization, and some proposed organizational and leadership changes.

The search process began in earnest in the early fall. I had interviews with the search firm and the board's search committee. The process was moving along when the next announcement was made: We would be selling the company to Charles Schwab.

While the sale announcement was a surprise, it was not a shock to me. From my vantage point, I had witnessed the company's challenges mounting. Schwab had recently reduced stock trading commissions to zero, interest rates remained stubbornly low, new entrants were changing the trading and investing landscape, consumers were looking for a more holistic financial services provider, and TD Ameritrade had never fully optimized the relationship with our strategic partner, TD Bank. Now we lacked a permanent CEO.

Schwab had made it very difficult for TD Ameritrade to remain independent by taking trading commissions to zero. For its part, TD Ameritrade lacked the broad revenue and product diversification, along with the necessary scale, to remain independent. Consequently, it was the board's judgment that this was the best time to sell the company to Charles Schwab.

The sale of Scottrade to TD Ameritrade in 2016, the sale of TD Ameritrade to Charles Schwab in 2019, and the sale of E*TRADE to Morgan Stanley in February of 2020, effectively meant the end of the discount brokerage industry, at least the one I knew. From my seat at the table at two of these three transactions, the end was predictable. It was a matter of when, not if, consolidation would occur.

The deal announcement was a shock to our associates. As was the case at Scottrade, many TD Ameritrade associates were fiercely loyal long-term employees. In addition, the company had been built through acquisitions: they were accustomed to being the acquirers, not the acquired. This fact made it even more difficult to comprehend that an era was ending.

I have long been an admirer of Charles Schwab—the person and the company. Schwab was the obvious partner for TD Ameritrade. The companies had common roots but had taken divergent paths over time. Neither path was wrong; they were just different.

Schwab had become a full-service financial services firm with a diversified set of financial products and services while TD Ameritrade had focused primarily on trading. Schwab's diversification into banking, managed investments, proprietary investment products, and the RIA custody space had served them well. They became a strong, well-diversified, consistent performer through different market and economic cycles.

Schwab has always been extremely well managed with a clear and consistent client-centered strategy. Schwab is a public company, unlike

Scottrade and Fidelity which were privately held. Charles Schwab himself remained active in setting the firm's strategic direction. His values and belief systems still permeate the company. No major decision has escaped his review.

Throughout my career, I have worked for two public companies (UMB and TD Ameritrade), and three private companies (Lockwood/Friedman, Fidelity Investments, and Scottrade). In many respects, UMB and Schwab were hybrids in the sense that the Kemper family still had primary oversight over UMB, and Charles Schwab remains a major force at Schwab. These founder-leaders were the glue that ensured that long-held beliefs and values remained in place even as the organizations and the times changed.

I have come to appreciate that while a company's structure matters, its leadership is the more important element. At a time in which the average tenure of a public company CEO is approximately five years, founder-led or founder-influenced companies tend to have more stability and a better sense of who they are and what they stand for. When your last name is essentially over the front door, there is bound to be a higher standard of care. The brand is shared—part the company's and part the individual's. The two are inseparable. Founder-leaders ensure continuity of purpose and foster an appreciation for how the company got to where it is. They are fully aware that trust takes years to build and seconds to lose.

With the ink dry on the $26 billion agreement to sell the company, the recruiting process for a new CEO ended. I was disappointed. The board decided to ask Steve Boyle, TD Ameritrade's CFO, to be the interim CEO until we could close the transaction, which would take almost a year. Steve was a good choice. He had the trust and confidence of the board, and his deep relationships with leaders at TD Bank made the transition easier for all concerned. In times of change, it is always better to limit the number of variables. This was one variable that would lessen the amount of disruption. The organization was about to go through a lot of disruption anyway. There would be difficult days ahead.

Throughout the fall, we started preliminary discussions with our new Schwab partners about integration planning. We had a few meetings, but we needed to be careful because we had not yet received full regulatory approval for the deal.

In early 2020, the global COVID-19 pandemic began. I remember my last trip was to Omaha for integration planning meetings. Within days, the entire country would be in a lockdown, the likes of which none of us had ever experienced. Almost without warning, we would need to shift our organization from an in-office position to a fully virtual one. Our primary concern was the health and safety of our associates and customers.

Not only did we have to run the organization in the COVID-19 environment, we also had to continue to progress on the deal integration plan. I was fortunate that my Schwab partner, Jonathan Craig, was a long-time Schwab leader. Jonathan understood the Schwab culture and organization, which would be extremely helpful in the weeks and months ahead as our two teams collaborated on integration planning.

Jonathan and I quickly came to respect each other and determined that we would collaborate to keep the ball rolling. Over the next nine months, we built a thoughtful integration plan. While we did not always agree on the path forward, I recognized that Schwab had acquired TD Ameritrade, and not the other way around. I understood that I ultimately needed to defer to Jonathan's views.

During the course of our integration planning, the pandemic continued to rage. With the exception of two in-person meetings prior to the pandemic's onset, we conducted the entire integration planning effort virtually, with Jonathan in San Francisco and me in St. Louis or Cape Cod. One day in the summer when Jonathan called to discuss an important matter, I was out kayaking with Michelle. I picked up the phone and spent the next hour talking to him from a kayak in the middle of Pleasant Bay. I don't think he ever knew that, nor did he need to.

If you had told me prior to the pandemic and the advent of a virtual workplace environment that the two teams would have been able to pull off the multi-billion-dollar transaction nearly flawlessly, I never would have believed it. Everyone did his or her best to build relationships and trust in the process, but virtual connections can only go so far. I missed the human connection with the Schwab team and my own team. We were able to successfully pull off the transaction, but we weren't able to build the deep relationships we otherwise would have. Even so, we closed the transaction in October 2020, with most of the business transacted online.

Once the deal was closed in early October, I was severed from TD Ameritrade. As part of my separation, I was asked to sign a two-year noncompete agreement, which I did. It was now time to determine the next chapter of my professional life with the knowledge that I could not work in the financial services industry, which had been my home for more than thirty years. I would need to find a new path forward.

I remember the strange feeling that came over me when I realized that I would not be in a meaningful leadership role for the first time in decades. It felt exceedingly strange. I had not yet completely processed what all this would mean to me. I realized my platform was about to disappear.

Months prior to the severance announcement, I had undertaken an extensive process of soul-searching to be prepared for this scenario. I reached out to recruiters about possible corporate leadership and board assignments. I thought long and hard about a stint in politics, something I had wanted to do for some time and had considered in the past. I thought I might get into consulting. I might ramp up my nonprofit work, about which I am passionate. There were many options, but no clear path readily emerged.

The only thing I knew for sure was that I was nowhere near ready for that dreaded word *retirement*. Crosby Kemper Jr. had once remarked that retirement was "God's waiting room." I was certainly not ready for that. I still had a lot of energy and much to give to others. I remembered my mother saying that you are going to sleep a long time when you are dead, so arrive tired.

Of course, there were family considerations, whichever direction I might choose. I had promised Michelle that if I did not move forward with Schwab, we would determine the next chapter together. While we had always made important decisions together, Michelle had compromised her interests and career for my career several times. Whatever the next step, there had to be something in it for Michelle. I really wanted to find a way forward that would be mutually beneficial and supportive of our thirty-plus-year relationship.

Chapter 10

Navigating Life's Third Chapter: Harvard University

At just under sixty, some might have chosen to retire. I had seen other friends and colleagues about my age do so. But not me. I was still vibrant, full of potential, and full of the desire to learn more, give back more, and be more. I thought I was nearing the pinnacle of my career and instead found myself in a valley. In short order, I needed to come to terms with my new reality.

The most difficult adjustment was accepting that I was no longer connected to a corporate platform. In my role as a C-suite executive, my corporate persona was deeply intertwined with my personal persona. Looking back even now, it's hard to tell which persona dominated. Perhaps they grew together as I matured.

My corporate platform allowed me to have a voice, a place, and a megaphone to speak and be heard. That voice first emerged in full strength for me in the community work I undertook in Kansas City as a senior executive at UMB.

The UMB platform had enabled me to speak with a measure of authority and credibility to positively influence events around me. It allowed me to allocate resources to the things I cared about and that were in alignment with the organization's business and social mission. The platform provided a pathway to make a difference in the lives of others. Essentially, my UMB platform and the others that followed provided a way for me to be relevant in my community. It was never about me; it was always about the good that I and others could do. I was fully aware of the power and responsibility that went along with my platform.

Suddenly, I was an executive without a corporate framework behind me, a community advocate without a corporate platform or its expansive resources. Almost overnight, the calls and emails asking for advice, counsel, and decisions stopped. I was no longer relevant to my former colleagues and community in the way I had previously been.

It wasn't that I hadn't realized this would happen, but the speed and force of it was nearly enough to knock me off my feet. It felt as if I had never existed in my prior context. Sure, there were terrific memories and much to be proud of, but suddenly I felt like no one needed my help any longer. Even my two daughters were grown and off on their own. It was an eerie, displaced kind of feeling.

The deep, mutually beneficial relationships I built up over time continued unabated. As time passed, I could better understand with whom I had a true, long-term, mutually beneficial relationship and with whom relationships were more transactional, short-term, or situational.

As a realist and a planner, I had started thinking about what might be next. Going back into the financial industry was not going to be a near-term possibility. I was going to need to remain flexible, consider different pathways, and take some risks. I was going to need to call on my inner Gumby.

My colleague Lauren States suggested I look into the Harvard University Advanced Leadership Initiative (ALI). Lauren, a 2015 ALI Fellow, talked glowingly about the transformational nature of her experience in the program.

The description on the ALI website caught my attention:

> The Advanced Leadership Initiative Fellowship is designed to enhance and leverage the skills of highly accomplished, experienced

leaders who want to apply their talents to solve significant social problems, including those affecting health and welfare, children and the environment, and focus on community and public service in the next phase of their careers.

I wasn't sure if I was ready to make a complete career pivot to social impact work exclusively. But I liked the fact that the ALI program focused on advanced leadership and offered an alternative lens through which to view seemingly intractable, wicked global social issues. The thought of being at Harvard and interacting with all those brainiacs was exciting too.

I learned that the ALI program has several appealing dimensions. It includes participation in a learning cohort comprising the other Fellows. These Fellows, originating from all over the world, are leaders in their respective fields, including business, law, education, health care, government, nonprofits, public service, and the arts. Each participant is selected because of his or her accomplishments, passion for leadership, and desire to give back.

In addition to a comprehensive ALI cohort curriculum, ALI participants are invited to audit as many courses as they can handle across the various schools at the university. I had always wanted to take courses in Harvard's John F. Kennedy School of Government to scratch my political itch, and at Harvard Business School to further refine my leadership skills. To do so without the requirement of completing papers or taking exams was attractive. I had never thought much about the other schools, but I began to think that they were equally likely to offer courses that would provide eye-opening experiences.

As I was researching the program, I thought the opportunity to build relationships with current and past cohort members, along with professors and other members of the Harvard community, might be enough to justify the program's time and effort. When I reviewed the list of the previous year's Fellows, however, I became instantly intimidated.

The individuals were all so accomplished. Two participants hailed from the United Nations while another had spent twenty years at the US Department of Justice. Another was Zambia's ambassador to the United Nations, while another led Amazon's books and entertainment media businesses. Did I belong alongside such accomplished individuals? I wasn't at all sure. A rush of past insecurities came flowing back. Still, I kept investigating.

Participating in ALI would allow Michelle and me to move back to our native Boston, closer to our two daughters and other friends and family members, after living in the Midwest for seventeen years. That would be a great benefit.

Another benefit, however, was the one that tipped the scales in the program's favor. ALI invites the spouse or significant other of the participating Fellow to fully participate in the program. Many of these partners are highly accomplished as well.

This is brilliant on Harvard's part, considering that the participants and their significant others come from all over the world. Participation makes the decision to relocate to Cambridge for a time easier, and it allows those individuals to be truly involved and engaged. Michelle and I could go through the program together.

Michelle was excited about this opportunity. Participation would give her a strong sense of purpose since she would once again be leaving her community work and friendships in St. Louis. She had made a significant impact helping to grow the St. Louis Community Foundation and had served on the boards of St. Louis Children's Hospital and St. Louis Public Radio.

After going where we needed to go for my career over the past thirty years, we could now do something together, something that would tap into the talents and interests of each of us. This was something Michelle and I could have fun with. Together. We decided to do it. There was just one small detail: I had to convince Harvard that I was a good candidate.

The admissions process was challenging and given the uncertainties about the continuance of my career at Charles Schwab right up until I was officially severed, I was late to apply for admission to the 2021 cohort. I was initially told that my application would be considered for admission to the 2022 cohort. I politely told Mike Emery, who leads the ALI admissions process, that 2022 would not work for me. I could not afford to spend precious time waiting to join the program. After some internal discussion, the admissions team was kind enough to consider me for the 2021 cohort.

Over the next two weeks, I completed the application and interviews with members of the ALI staff and faculty advisors. After a fair amount of back and forth, more interviews, and writing a ten-page paper on the social impact project I was considering, I was accepted into the 2021 ALI cohort, which began on January 2, 2021.

Because COVID-19 was still spreading, the entire first semester's programming would be conducted virtually. This was completely understandable. I wondered how online engagement was going to work with individuals I had no prior connection to, but I thought, This is Harvard; surely, they will figure it out.

Shortly after I was accepted, our daughter, Sarah, took us for a walk around Harvard Yard and Harvard Square to familiarize us with the university grounds. That was somewhat surreal; it had not been too long before that Michelle and I had dropped our daughters off at their colleges of choice. Now in our late fifties, we were entering another college experience of our own.

Although I was genuinely excited about attending Harvard and expected it to be a real stretch, I knew that the program would not help me stay connected and keep me relevant in the corporate world during the two-year noncompete period. I had always run hard, and I wanted to keep on running. I recognized that two years would be up quickly, and that Harvard would be over before I knew it. I needed to prepare for life after Harvard before even beginning.

Because I didn't know exactly what I wanted to do next, I was determined to create as many options for myself as possible. It's always a good practice to have multiple options so that if one door closes, another might open. Billionaire investor and businessman Charlie Munger once said that the "fundamental algorithm of life is to repeat what works." This approach had always worked for me, so that is what I did. I accepted admission to the ALI program; became a board member of four private companies and a few nonprofit organizations in addition to those on which I was already serving; continued serving as a trustee for a large family foundation; and carved out time to write this book. In addition, Michelle and I made time to reconnect. We took several family trips and enjoyed our summers together on Cape Cod.

> **Board Positions Come through Multiple Channels**
>
> Many people ask me how to find board opportunities. I explain that this is a process rather than an event. The cultivation process is constantly in motion. It is hard work that needs to be treated almost as a full-time job. Begin with the fundamentals:
>
> - Ensure that your LinkedIn profile is up to date and representative of how you wish to be portrayed
> - Create a board-specific bio and résumé
> - Identify specific target organizations
> - Develop a network of recruiters
> - Leverage your business and personal relationships
> - Join the National Association of Corporate Directors (NACD) even if you have not yet secured your first board position
> - Complete the NACD Directorship Certification program
>
> During my first few months at Harvard, I discovered four wonderful board opportunities, through various channels.
>
> My first new corporate board assignment came through LinkedIn. I do not usually respond to requests to connect from people I do not know. However, a request from Miguel García Ruiz caught my attention. Miguel is the co-CEO of Infosel, an information, data, and technology company headquartered in Mexico.
>
> Ordinarily, that might have been enough for me to dismiss the request. But upon some additional company research, I became intrigued by the nature of the company and its growth prospects in South America.

Miguel had reached out believing that my experience with leading large investment and investment services platforms could be helpful to them. After several interviews with other investors and management, I was asked to join the board.

The second opportunity came through a former board member at Scottrade. Claire Huang called to see if I was interested in discussing the possibility of joining the board of Prosper Marketplace. Prosper is one of the original fintech peer-to-peer lending organizations, based in San Francisco. Claire was kind enough to recommend me to the CEO, David Kimball, who thought my operational and client service background would be helpful. I went through an exhaustive interview process and was asked to join the board.

The next opportunity, with Edelman Financial Engines, came through the traditional recruiter channel. The company was looking for someone who had deep knowledge of financial services and had successfully led large sales and service organizations. I had long admired founder Ric Edelman and the great brand and business he created. I was thrilled to be considered for this opportunity. There was, however, one complication. Given the potential competitive nature with Schwab, I would need to get clearance from Schwab prior to accepting any appointment. Schwab could not have been nicer: They granted the waiver.

The final board opportunity was referred to me by a friend, Horacio Marquez. Horacio and I met in Florida at a sailing regatta in which our daughters competed some years earlier. We sailed together during the event and had kept in touch over the years. This opportunity would be initially to engage with a company called Onepak, an emerging leader in reverse logistics. Over time, I became an investor and board member.

The important message in these stories is that finding board opportunities takes a multichannel approach. Infosel found me through LinkedIn. I was referred to Prosper by a former colleague. A traditional recruiter reached out to me for the Edelman Financial Engines opportunity, and an acquaintance who had become a friend introduced me to the fourth. Another important trait is that these are all private companies. I have found it much easier to find private board opportunities than

> public company opportunities. Private company boards, which I have found easier to navigate, also come with a lot less scrutiny than public company boards.

The Harvard ALI program started in earnest virtually in January 2021. As with the previous year's cohort, our cohort was comprised of leaders of national and global consequence, along with noted national business and social impact leaders. Some of the best minds in academia would be working with our cohort.

Since the entire first semester was going to be conducted online, Michelle and I decided to spend some time in Florida, taking our classes from there, which was not a bad way to attend Harvard. Fortunately, we were able to resume somewhat normal on-campus activities for the second and third semesters, although masks were required, and social gatherings were strongly discouraged.

As the program got underway, it was still unclear to me how the members of our fifty-person cohort were going to build trust and relationships over the internet. The ALI leadership team tried mightily to have each of us engage with the others to build the bonds of friendship. There were virtual breakout sessions and opportunities for virtual social interactions. Even so, the interactions were still difficult and largely transactional.

From the start, the cohort tackled some of the most difficult social issues of our time, including racism, climate change, challenges to democracy, the impact of social media, and the power of technology to transform human existence.

Quickly, the discussions became strained. Some voices drowned out others; some shut down and chose not to participate. The difficulty was never an issue of malice, only the challenge of discussing highly charged emotional topics without the benefit of extended time together to build relationships and trust. Each person brought his or her own unique life experiences to the table. In one instance, a cohort member was challenged for her perspectives on racism after a somewhat controversial presentation. Her perspectives had come from her lived experiences, which others did not fully understand or appreciate.

Another early challenge was that some cohort members thought that in the absence of in-person contact, cross-cohort communication by email would be a suitable venue for deep dialogue and debate. This also proved challenging. While email is a proper medium for some communication types, it is not a good medium in which to have difficult, emotionally charged conversations.

The lack of context, perspective, body language, and the inability to have a dynamic conversation made for some difficult early discussions. We were a microcosm of a world that was struggling to understand this new virtual existence. We had to determine how to uncover the humanity in others, build relationships, and counter the tendency to view others as merely one-dimensional images in boxes on a Zoom screen.

Despite the challenges of the classes being fully virtual, I found the moderated conversations helpful as different perspectives were presented, informed by others' lived experiences. This opened my eyes to new ways of thinking about old problems. While I did not agree with all the new perspectives, it was a powerful learning experience for me.

In contrast to the first semester, the second semester was held on the Harvard campus, with a hybrid option for those who felt more comfortable continuing to participate virtually. We began the semester with a two-day facilitated session. This was the first time we had the opportunity to meet each other in person and begin the process of developing friendships, relationships, perspective, and trust.

Immediately upon gathering, the feeling in the cohort shifted. Gone were the static images of individuals sitting alone in their remote locations from around the globe. In its place, real human beings were laughing, building friendships, developing relationships, and having a good time being together.

Some of the individuals seemed exactly as they presented themselves on Zoom; others seemed entirely different. In one case, I had thought from Zoom that one of our cohort members was a large, imposing figure, only to realize that she was, in fact, tiny in stature, but still a powerful force. I wondered what others thought of me now that they could meet me in person.

These first few days of the second semester reminded me about the necessity for and value of human contact in creating, understanding, and appreciating differing perspectives; solving problems and leveraging diversity; and just plain enjoying each other's company.

For thirty-plus years, I had been thinking of the difficult problems I tackled through my own lived experiences and through the lens of a business leader, someone whose primary goal to was run a successful business enterprise. The new perspectives the cohort members offered were a powerful reminder that all vantage points must be considered when seeking to solve difficult problems.

Conceiving, preparing, and presenting a social impact project is one of the central learning experiences of the ALI program. When I applied to the program, my social impact paper proposal was about creating an economic renaissance on the Massachusetts South Coast. I had contributed to the economic renaissance in Kansas City, and I thought I could replicate that success in my hometown region.

The South Coast is a part of Massachusetts that has underperformed economically since the textile mills, which were once the epicenter of the local economy, migrated to the South. While light manufacturing and making a living from the sea are still important industries in the region, they have not been enough to propel the local economy forward. When I graduated from college, opportunities were few and far between. I had to leave the region to pursue my dreams. I wanted greater opportunities for others.

I set out to do this by leveraging my new cohort relationships, relationships with professors, and my social impact learnings at Harvard. As part of my research, I visited with the dean of the business school at UMass Dartmouth (my alma mater), the co-CEOs of the SouthCoast Chamber of Commerce, the leader of Entrepreneurship for All (EforAll), and other influential local business and civic leaders.

One day, as Michelle and I were talking, she asked me if I was passionate about my ALI social impact project. I told her that I was excited about it and thought that I could make a positive contribution. She listened and then asked, "Peter, why the heck aren't you making your social impact project about CMT? You have all the resources of Harvard and the ALI cohort at your disposal. You will never have this opportunity again. Carpe diem. Seize the day!"

Her challenge hit me hard, and I knew immediately that Michelle was right. After a lifetime of stubborn silence about my CMT, it was time to go public; it was time to become a leader in the fight to find treatments and cures for the disease.

Two events occurred over the previous few years to bring about this change in me. One was a significant change brought about by Pat Livney, with whom I had been friends over the past decade. Pat, as I described in Chapter 5, had been the CEO of the Charcot-Marie-Tooth Association. By this time he had become disenfranchised with the organization.

Pat felt that while the CMTA was doing great work providing a myriad of resources—camps for children, regional support groups, and access to medical providers treating symptoms of the disease—the organization wasn't investing enough to find treatments and potential cures.

In 2018, Pat left the CMTA to co-found, with Susan Ruediger, the CMT Research Foundation (CMTRF). The organization focuses on raising funds for and investing in the most promising CMT research. According to its website, "The CMT Research Foundation is a patient-led, non-profit focused solely on delivering treatments and cures for Charcot-Marie-Tooth disease." The specificity resonated with me. Pat came to me once again, asking me to join his board and consider going public.

Second, it became harder and harder to ignore the impact of CMT on my extended family. My sister, Lynne; my daughter, Sarah; my niece, Amy; my brothers; and other nephews and nieces were all suffering at an increased intensity. My long-held position had become untenable.

With Pat whispering in my ear, my family's struggle with the disease, and Michelle's bold encouragement, I chose to work toward creating awareness and raising funds to seek treatments and cures for CMT. This would be my social impact project. It was my destiny.

I finally no longer cared what anyone thought of me in terms of my disease. I'd had a reasonable degree of success in life, and I was going to try to parlay that into helping people with CMT. As a start, I joined the CMTRF board of directors.

The CMTRF is an excellent example of what can happen when an organization or individual is focused. Not long after I joined the board, Pat asked me to chair a $10 million fundraising campaign to fund research on CMT1-A, the most prevalent form of CMT and the one that runs in my family. For an organization that was less than three years old and had only raised about $5 million over the preceding three years, raising $10 million seemed like a tall order. Still, I said yes.

Susan Ruediger, who is a fellow-sufferer of CMT1-A, is my partner on this campaign. Susan had been working in and around CMT fundraising and research for the better part of fifteen years by the time we first met. She was well known in the research and scientific circles as a mover and a shaker.

Together, Susan and I determined that the best approach would be to think of the fundraising target as a series of concentric circles. Those in the innermost circles are patients and patients' families. The next concentric circle consists of friends of those afflicted. After that are those who are connected to those who are afflicted with CMT. These circles continue expanding outward until you get to the point where the individuals in the outer circles have no connection to the disease itself or anyone afflicted with the disorder.

The best chance for early fundraising success would be to penetrate the innermost circles. While these are not the largest circles in terms of donor numbers, we believed that this group would be the most willing to fund the research since there would be a direct or indirect benefit. These were and are the individuals who have the most at stake.

We launched the campaign at the CMT Global Research Convention, which was the first one in its history, in September 2021. The convention was held virtually as the pandemic was still limiting the ability to gather in person.

Over the two-day convention, over one hundred researchers and three hundred patients attended the conference to hear about the latest worldwide research to uncover treatments and cures for CMT. While there had been progress and many exciting developments to report, there was not yet an approved treatment.

During the convention, Susan and I hosted a campaign fundraising Zoom event. After the researchers gave a status update on potential drug development, the most amazing thing began to happen as prospective donors came forward to commit to the campaign. Encouraged by the research and the singular focus of our campaign, over $3 million was raised that night alone. Over the next few weeks, as we made our follow-up calls and pitches, we tallied over $4.5 million in contributions. We were on our way to $10 million.

For once, I felt like I was making a difference in the advancement of treatments and cures of CMT. It felt great. I just wished I had started sooner. As the saying goes, better late than never.

Fundraising Alone Will Never Bring About Needed Social Change

Businesses are powerful platforms. Over 160 million people are employed by US businesses. The things that happen inside these businesses, the cultures that are created, and the way associates, clients and customers are treated influence more than just the bottom line.

The platforms conferred on business leaders empower them to promote a message, start a conversation, create a culture, or focus resources on important social causes. Often the focus is on what is good for the business and the broader community.

When used effectively, business platforms can be a powerful force for driving positive societal change. Effective utilization requires strong moral purpose; bold, powerful messaging; and the willingness to tackle controversial problems, which can lead to long-term systemic change and business success.

Absent or irresponsible use of a business platform can have long-reaching effects as well. An example of irresponsible use of power is the historical practice of banking "redlining." In this practice, communities of color were systematically underinvested in, the result of which has been a lack of generational wealth creation in marginalized communities. The effects of redlining continue to echo loudly today.

I was working at UMB when I first understood the power of using business platforms for social good. At first, I assumed my platform was just a mechanism to raise money for organizations, nothing more. I chaired many events, made lots of calls to other business leaders asking for resources, wrote checks, and breathed a sigh of relief when we exceeded our fundraising goals. I made my contribution by raising funds and moving on from one fundraising endeavor to another. I didn't appreciate that there was anything else I was accountable to do.

Over time, I came to realize that platforms require constant attention and activation to remain vital resources for advancing the common good. These platforms are destined to be underutilized if they are solely about fundraising and money or self-serving messages.

Corporate and community leadership requires full-contact engagement, emanating from many different sides and angles. This includes listening, fundraising, advocacy, community engagement, championing causes, giving a voice, and even aligning brands when appropriate. The full mobilization of people, finances, and resources must come together persistently in common cause.

One day, Bernard Franklin walked into my office in Kansas City. Bernard was the relatively new president of Junior Achievement of Middle America (JAMA). UMB had been a partner of JAMA for some time, providing direct funding and hosting an annual bowl-a-thon fundraiser. While Bernard was grateful for UMB's past financial support, money was not his focus on this visit.

Bernard wanted to discuss how we could create a deeper partnership with more direct person-to-person engagement, one that would be of mutual benefit to the people of both organizations. He sought a partnership in which UMB associates could actively participate in the effort beyond just throwing bowling balls at pins once a year. We needed to align the two organization's brands, missions and people.

I asked K. C. Mathews, UMB Bank's Chief Investment Officer, to lead the effort. K. C. went to work and engaged the entire Kansas City UMB workforce. Our associates responded with enthusiasm, not because anyone told them they needed to but because they were part of a culture of giving and caring. Our associates felt the responsibility to engage. Their participation was a manifestation of UMB's solid commitment to always "do the right thing" for its community.

We also placed dozens of associates in classrooms, teaching the principles of business and free enterprise to students across the region.

I have learned many lessons over my thirty-five years of leading business and community organizations. One of the most important is that those in positions of leadership and authority have a voice. They have the obligation to speak up and speak out on behalf of those who can't do so for themselves. With leadership comes great responsibility to speak out when injustice occurs, when truth has been squelched, or when a simple misunderstanding might lead to unnecessary conflict.

Leaders must engage more with those with whom they disagree. They must embrace the notion of listening to others and seeking to understand before taking action.

Recently, I received an email from Bernard. Since his days at JAMA, Bernard has been a leader in higher education and, coincidentally, became a 2022 Harvard ALI Fellow. His email touched a chord when he wrote the following:

> Your people [UMB] were always there in full force, fully engaged and fully present. I asked some of the loan officers and other leadership about the UMB cultural environment . . . they said you were building a culture of involvement not just with dollars to the community but with the bank employees' presence and commitment. This is a reflection of your leadership and your commitment to serving every diverse Kansas City community. The Latino and African-American communities were so grateful for the support and the assistance UMB provided the community. All we had to do was call and ask, and the rest was done. There is still lots to be done, but you helped to create grocery stores, expand housing projects, etc.

While Bernard gives me way too much credit, his statement is a testimony to the leadership platform UMB, the Greater Kansas City Chamber of Commerce, the Civic Council of Greater Kansas City, and many other business and civic organizations used to create a culture of positive change and engagement, the effects of which will be felt by individuals for years to come in that wonderful Midwestern city.

In today's digitally-led world, genuine, authentic, face-to-face, and mutually beneficial relationships remain the cornerstone of human thriving. Real understanding and reconciliation can only begin through direct human engagement with those who differ from us. Do not be tricked into believing that money is the answer or that engaging with others virtually is an adequate substitute for face-to-face contact or relationships. The person-to-person approach is a necessary ingredient to transform this world into a better place.

At least three challenges are inherent in fundraising for a rare disease like CMT. The first is the lack of broad awareness and a brand with which prospective donors can identify. Even though there are at least three million cases of CMT globally (making it the most common of a category called "rare diseases"), most people do not know about it. There are no national spokespersons (as Michael J. Fox is for Parkinson's, the late Jerry Lewis was for the Muscular Dystrophy Association, or Lou Gehrig was for the disease that bears his name.)

The second challenge is that because CMT is generally not life-threatening or life-shortening, it falls closer to the bottom of the federal government's public health priorities. Contrast that with diseases such as AIDS, cancer, or COVID-19, which warrant all-out assaults and billions of dollars in spending from the federal government. While some funding is provided for CMT, it is nowhere near enough to seriously fund the research necessary to unlock effective treatments and cures.

The third challenge is a lack of coordination on a global level. Only 5 percent of the individuals affected by CMT live in the US. That means that 95 percent, in terms of patients and prospective donors, reside outside the US. Any successful effort with respect to the fundraising and research must be global in nature.

One morning in the fall of 2021, Susan sent me a link to a television appearance by country music superstar Alan Jackson that had aired that morning. To my surprise and dismay, Alan had just announced in a *Today* show interview with Jenna Bush Hager that he was suffering from CMT.

I sat and watched the video a few times to make sure I heard right. Here was the great Alan Jackson revealing that he had the same condition I did. I was not alone anymore. Here is some of what Alan said:

> I have this neuropathy and neurological disease . . . it's genetic . . . that I inherited from my daddy. There's no cure for it, but it's been affecting me for years. And it's getting more and more obvious. And I know I'm stumbling around on stage. And now I'm having

a little trouble balancing, even in front of the microphone, and so I just feel very uncomfortable.

He went on to add:

It's not going to kill me. It's not deadly, but it's related [to] muscular dystrophy and Parkinson's disease . . . I don't want people to be sad for me; it's part of life . . . I've had a wonderful, beautiful life. I've been so blessed. It's just good to put it out there in the open. In some ways, it's a relief.

I share Alan's sentiments. It is a relief to have it out there.

As I was working on my social impact project, I was also participating in the ALI work, taking classes in different schools at Harvard, and building relationships with others in the cohort.

Over time, certain members of the cohort gravitated toward others. In some instances, the attraction came from the comfort of aligning with individuals who, perhaps, looked like them, thought like them, or had similar life experiences. This is natural.

In my case, I made a conscious effort to expand beyond my comfort zone. I sought out other perspectives and built amazing new friendships, each of which broadened my thinking.

Tim Merrill, an education advocate, youth leadership developer, counselor, mentor, and pastor from Camden, New Jersey, is an example. One of the organizations Tim founded is Watu Moja, a global service program for Camden's African-American and Afro-Latino young adults.

Tim spoke eloquently about the challenges of today's African-American youth in Camden's inner city. He talked about how poverty, racism, joblessness, community disinvestment, and fear formed the nexus of their experiences. This was the world these individuals lived and the lens through which they judged the world.

Over time, Tim and I became great friends. We shared our unique experiences respectfully and at times cordially agreed to disagree. I have grown through my friendship with Tim. In fact, Michelle asked Tim to offer a blessing at my sixtieth birthday party, which was a beautiful gift for me.

Another new friend was John Elser. John has been a highly successful businessperson, and he and his wife, Jeanne, were in the ALI program as were Michelle and I. That gave us a special bond. We had deep conversations about many things and challenged each other. John and I became quick friends. Like everyone in the program, John was on a journey aided by the new perspectives being offered by the other cohort members. I was grateful to be on the road with him.

Also, there was Yinka Omorogbe, who hails from Nigeria. Yinka served as the second-ever female attorney general and justice commissioner in Edo State, Nigeria, where she also chaired Edo's task force against human trafficking. She brought a fascinating global perspective to our discussions. Each time Yinka spoke, I listened intently, eager to tease out a nugget of wisdom. Yinka's insights about the world, and especially Africa's place in it, had a deep impact on me and my perspectives.

It was Yinka who introduced me to the idea of how the continent of Africa is represented as smaller than it really is on many maps. The map we are all most familiar with is the Mercator projection, which was developed in 1569 by European cartographer Geert de Kremer. This representation greatly distorts the relative areas of land masses. It makes Africa look small and Greenland and Russia appear larger than they are. There is a new map called the Peters Projection map with equal area representation that is gaining acceptance. In fact, the Boston Public Schools recently introduced this map into their curriculum. Yinka's pointing this out gave me new knowledge about Africa's place in the world and how important it is to Africans that their continent be represented properly to the rest of the world.

In a similar fashion, I was touched when Haifa Dia Al-Attia, an accomplished educational consultant from Jordan, shared her perspective about the Palestinian and Israeli conflict and, from her experience, spoke about the pain and suffering on both sides. Haifa's comments were apolitical, remarks from someone who yearns for peace in a region that has seen too much war and suffering for too long.

Fellow Linda Rebrovick from Nashville, Tennessee quickly became a trusted friend. Because of that trust, I confided in her early on about my struggle with CMT. She was supportive and wanted to see how she might help. Linda was the first one to reach out to me after Alan Jackson announced his battle with CMT.

Linda, who had previously run for mayor of Nashville, took it upon herself to reach out to Alan Jackson's team to see if a partnership might be struck between the country music star and the CMTRF. I was floored by her willingness to get involved without being asked. I began to realize just how much others would respond to my being open about my CMT.

My time at Harvard and with the ALI program opened my eyes to the power of lived experiences. According to *Oxford Reference*, lived experiences are the "personal knowledge about the world gained through direct, firsthand involvement in everyday events rather than through representations constructed by other people." I grew as a person because I interacted with the members of our cohort. It reminded me that each perspective is unique and enriches the other. My encounters with these individuals have enriched and added depth and dimension to my mosaic.

When the 2021 ALI cohort was first announced, I was pleased to see the cohort's diversity. I had expected racial and ethnic diversity, but that was only the beginning. Complex issues were explored through a variety of different lenses, including leadership, business, and community advocacy. This experience began to remind me of the unintended bigotry I experienced early in life because my ancestry and battle with CMT made me different. It took some time, but eventually I was able to overcome that bigotry and become who I am now.

Opening oneself to such a wide range of diverse perspectives is not for the faint of heart. It would have been easy to close my mind to all this stimulus and maintain my traditional way of thinking. That, however, would be to stop learning and growing, closing myself off to one of my main goals in participating in the program.

The important thing throughout the ALI experience was to remain open to the possibility that even my long-held ideas might be incomplete, misinformed, or even wrong. I appreciated that there were other ways to look at any situation or a problem. It was not my place to judge, but to listen, ask questions, and seek to understand. I have come to appreciate that strength is derived from vulnerability, and wisdom comes from experience—not a single experience, but the full lifetime of experiences of the people you encounter.

In addition to my work in the cohort, I took the opportunity to audit intellectually stimulating courses. These included "The Art and Adventures of Public Leadership" at the Harvard Kennedy School with former White House presidential advisor David Gergen. I took a course on American democracy with Cornel West, who is one of America's foremost philosophers and political activists. West is an outspoken voice in left-wing politics in the United States. His perspective is often radically different from mine. While I agreed with very little of what Professor West espoused, I loved every minute of the class.

I also took a course called "Corporate Responsibility and New Governance Models" with Jane Nelson, who is the director of the Corporate Responsibility Initiative at the Harvard Kennedy School. I audited a course called "The United States and China" with Professor William Kirby, one of the foremost thinkers in this critically important area, and one with Professor Pippa Norris called "The Rise of Authoritarian Populism," which was a deep dive into today's highly charged political environment. Each of the classes was intellectually stimulating, gave me new perspectives, and was highly relevant for leaders during these uncertain times. Each contributed insight and sparkle to my mosaic.

I sat in Harvard classes with undergraduate and graduate students who are a generation younger than me. I found the students passionate, brilliant, and accepting. Their thoughts and insights were formed by the experiences of their respective generations. Their perspectives came from their lived experiences and the perspectives of others on social media. This was neither good nor bad, just a reality.

Another of my fresh insights from my time at Harvard concerns the state of our environment and climate. I audited a class on climate change with Professor Dan Schrag, director of the Harvard University Center for the Environment. I appreciated his unemotional, factual, and science-based insights. I especially enjoyed working through his model detailing how various energy inputs from fossil fuels to solar and wind generation created different climate outcomes over time. Schrag's ability to make the complex simple, understandable, and relatable is his genius.

Michelle took many courses related to the environment, conservation, and environmental design, which are long-held passions for her. In addition to these classes, she went on excursions and became deeply involved with professors and other students.

On December 6, 2021, I delivered my social impact paper to the ALI cohort. I was nervous about presenting the paper in front of such an eminent group. While some of my cohort colleagues knew about my battle with CMT, others didn't.

The presentation was well received by the cohort, with many offering their assistance in any way possible. I was extremely gratified by the support and the response.

The months I spent at Harvard were an exhilarating time of personal growth. My time there renewed my appreciation for the university and for American higher education more broadly. It is undeniable that Harvard is one of the, if not the preeminent institution of higher learning in the United States.

It has the well-deserved reputation for having some of the brightest minds and sharpest thinkers across all its various schools and disciplines. Harvard professors and researchers publish some of the best scholarly research across a wide array of subject matter. The university recruits the finest students and educates them in a multidisciplinary, classic liberal arts fashion. I am a better, more well-rounded, better-informed leader and person exiting the program than I was upon entering.

Upon completing ALI, Michelle became a senior Fellow at the highly reputable Conservation Law Foundation (CLF) in Boston. The Conservation Law Foundation "protects New England's environment for the benefit of all people." CLF uses the law, science, and the market to create solutions that preserve natural resources, build healthy communities, and sustain a vibrant economy. Michelle started working with CLF to assess the success of their impact investment funds.

Following our completion of the ALI program, the fundraising campaign continued, and we made steady progress. Alan Jackson embarked on a concert tour called "Last Call: One More for the Road." The CMTRF worked with the tour, and Alan graciously committed to donate one dollar from every tour ticket sold to the CMTRF. It was a watershed event for the foundation. It helped to extend the Foundation's brand and, more important, the awareness of CMT.

I volunteered to host an event in Kansas City where I still had deep relationships from my time at UMB. I knew from prior experience that people give money to people as much as they give money to specific causes. I knew I still had enduring relationships in Kansas City. Maybe some of those colleagues and friends would want to help, but I would need to ask.

One friend, Roshann Parris, who is one of the shrewdest public relations executives in the country, suggested that for the event to be successful, I would need a few highly credible community and business leaders as event co-hosts. These individuals would need to be willing to put themselves out there with me and ask others for support. They would be placing their trust and confidence in me and my story.

I decided that we would need at least three co-hosts. I asked Cliff Illig, co-founder of Cerner Corporation; Terry Dunn, former CEO of JE Dunn Construction; and Karen Fenaroli, CEO of Fenaroli & Associates, if they would be willing to help. These are individuals with whom Michelle and I had built deep relationships when we lived in Kansas City. They are some of the pillars of the Kansas City business and philanthropic community and outstanding individuals.

I was nervous when I asked each of these individuals. They had no connection to the disease, only to Michelle and me, and we had not lived in Kansas City for almost seven years. Each said yes. Once again, the power of relationships and trust came through. Not only was this a testament to relationships, but a true testament to the generous leaders in that Midwestern community. We were on our way!

As we were planning the event, which included making a video that featured my story, a senior advisor to the CMTRF staff observed something that terrified me; the comment nearly caused me to back out altogether.

The individual said, "No one is going to feel sorry for you," and elaborated by saying that I couldn't be an effective spokesperson for the disease. I "looked too healthy," I "did not look sick enough," I "did not have enough of a physical handicap to motivate people to give."

While I walk with a limp and am in pain with every step, the manifestation of my disease—while still progressing—is currently in the moderate category. I have always hidden it well through limiting the types of recreation I undertake and the use of well-hidden braces and orthotics. Contrast that with the hundreds of thousands of people who live their lives in wheelchairs, use prosthetic devises to remain ambulatory, can't fully utilize their extremities, and have other visible and severe physical limitations.

At first, I was angry. What did this guy know? He did not suffer from the disease, although, unfortunately, his daughter did. Dwelling upon it further, I began to think that maybe he was right. Maybe I was the wrong person to represent the broader CMT community. Maybe the cause needed someone who more visibly bore the scars from the disease. But then it hit me: I am who I am, and I cannot change that. Fate gave me a moderate case of CMT. I did not need to apologize to anyone for fate.

Researchers recently told me that whatever treatments might emerge would be of no practical use to me. My disease has progressed too far. The damage is done. My efforts are for the next generation. Instead of depressing me, that notion inspired me. Too many have suffered for too long. This must end. Now.

Fate, along with hard work, also provided me with some deep relationships, the cognitive ability to formulate and articulate a message, compassion for others, and the desire to make an impact and leave a legacy. These were attributes that would be useful in raising funds to find treatments and cures. I could, and I would, stand up for everyone affected by this disease regardless of their CMT disease type and severity. There would be no turning around. No looking back.

The event was held in October 2022 at Mission Hills Country Club. Michelle was with me, supporting me all the way. More than thirty friends gathered to hear my story. As the four-minute video about my lifelong struggle with CMT played, I nervously finalized my thoughts.

This would be the first time I was fully transparent about my disease with this important group of people. There would be no more hiding behind an old injury and the other excuses I had used in the past.

I spoke about my lifetime of challenges in a highly personal way. I explained how hard it had been arriving at this moment. I asked for their patience and understanding as I spoke.

That evening we raised over $1.2 million, thanks to the incredible generosity of those assembled. One family with whom I have been associated for nearly twenty years pledged $1 million of that total amount. I was overwhelmed with emotion and gratitude.

The campaign had now raised $5.7 million in the first sixteen months. We were defying the fundraising analysts who said at the outset that it would be difficult for the campaign to raise even $5 million.

I had spent my entire life hiding behind my CMT, feeling emotions from shame to inferiority. I had finally conquered my demons. While I had never allowed CMT to define me, I had allowed it to affect me and the person I have become. The presentation of my ALI paper and my remarks at the fundraising event were more liberating than I can possibly say. I am now truly free of any misgivings about disclosing and openly talking about my CMT. I still have the physical manifestations to wrestle with; however, the powerful emotional baggage is finally gone.

I may or may not have a corporate platform in my life again. My next professional step has yet to be determined. I do, however, have a personal voice, a lifetime's worth of enduring relationships, and experience in bringing people together in support of a cause. Whatever comes next for me professionally, I'll continue in my personal commitment to use my strengths to leverage the CMTRF platform to uncover treatments and cures on behalf of all those affected by CMT. This will be a critical mission in my life's third chapter.

Chapter 11

Anticipating New Patterns of Growth: Wrapping Things Up

I remember the first time I used a fax machine at Fidelity Investments. Each afternoon we faxed the closing day's net asset value (NAV) for each of our mutual funds to NASDAQ and other distribution outlets so that our mutual fund prices could be published in the *Wall Street Journal* and other newspapers. I also remember the first IBM XT PC—with floppy disk technology—that a dozen of us shared across my department. I was a fledgling leader at the time. In December 2021, I hit the traumatic moment when I turned sixty. By then, some three decades past my joining Fidelity, my résumé listed multiple positions in the C-Suite.

From financial crises, market dislocations, and finally a global pandemic, my executive roles allowed me to participate in key business decisions and lead through adversity at critical moments. These were times of momentous change in the US and global markets, especially in the financial services industry.

The way businesses delivered their services changed dramatically during this time. Technology made everything move faster, drove massive increases in productivity, enhanced the total client experience, and made information ubiquitous. Data was transformed into information, which became transparent and easily accessible to everyone.

Much change was driven by rapid technological advancement, but some changes were driven by social changes, changing workforce demographics, and continually rising client and associate expectations. Employers and employees sought a better balance in their relationships. Long gone were the days when an associate went to work for a firm, was loyal to the firm, stayed for an extended period, and retired with a company-paid pension. Mobility became paramount.

Today, technology enables many to choose where to live first and where to work second, seeking a balance that eluded the generations before them. This is a major issue for every American city as leaders seek to make their community attractive to this mobile workforce. It is said that change is the only constant. I certainly experienced that throughout my thirty-five-year career.

My family threw a big sixtieth birthday party for me, with lots of family, close friends, and my new Harvard ALI colleagues. If my forced departure from the industry hadn't triggered me to take stock of my professional life, this milestone would have done so. Neither of these events signals the end of my professional and personal contributions, but they do mark a critical juncture. My energy level and drive to make a difference are still at full throttle.

As Michelle and I were working our way through the ALI program, I was also writing this book. A chance encounter at just the right time had prompted a decision to share what I had learned over my long career. Because I had a seat at the executive table at several financial service organizations during historic times, I believed I had a unique perspective to share. Most significant was the time I spent at UMB during the financial crisis. I was proud to be a member of an executive team that made decisions based on time-tested principled leadership when multiple forces pushed toward greed.

I had been intentionally working to define my own principles of effective leadership for years. During my season at Harvard, I wrestled with those principles in the pursuit of clarity. Were there nine, ten, or eleven? Could some be combined? What could I do to make each clearer? What could

I do to make them more succinct? This work was demanding, and it was months before I was satisfied with my list of ten.

Meanwhile, I was testing out the principles in my experiences in the ALI program. One of my biggest insights was the near-universal application of my principles in different contexts and environments.

For example, the principle to build enduring, mutually beneficial relationships is evergreen. It is applicable in every context. Another key principle is to engage, develop, and retain superior diverse talent. The ALI experience reinforced for me the power of diversity in all its forms. Our cohort's conversations were richer and deeper thanks to the diversity of experiences and views that were brought into the discussions. There were so many aha moments for me and other cohort members. We live in a world that is made more beautiful thanks to diversity. I hope and pray that we each learn to embrace it to the fullest.

I could go through all ten principles and recite how universally applicable they are, but I think you get the point.

During the process of writing the book, I had the realization that I wanted to title it *Taking Stock*. It occurred to me that this was exactly what I was doing. On multiple levels, the title just fit. What I didn't know at the time was that the book's name would shift my perspective, giving me more than I personally bargained for as I wrote.

For example, describing key relationships and encounters along my career path was an emotional experience. Leaders follow principles, but they do so in tandem with concern and support for others. I'd even say the best leaders follow principles in the context of love. If that's true, I've been fortunate to be very well loved.

Reflecting even now upon the compassion I received long ago at Cinema 140 from Roger Lockwood and Gordon McKinnon when being treated for kidney issues, I'm overcome with gratitude. The same is true when I think of the risk Fred Knapp quietly took when providing me with the opportunity to lead the turnaround at Fidelity's Covington facility. Fred never intended for me to know that he had stuck his neck out in a big way so that I could grow. These leaders earned my complete loyalty.

My parents were the first to instill values of honesty and integrity in me, but they weren't the last to do so. Integrity, practiced consistently throughout an organization, is contagious and self-perpetuating. How else can I explain how Crosby Kemper Jr. and those of us on his executive leadership team at UMB stood strong against pressure during the financial collapse? How can I explain the enduring impact of working around a principled giant like Ned Johnson and working directly for Rodger Riney?

Taking stock, it was hard to sidestep the lifelong tension that existed for me between the desire to be transparent and the deeply felt need to keep my medical condition private. Integrity pushed me to be honest, open, and approachable. I rationalized that this was a personal and private matter, not an intentional attempt to deceive. I sincerely strived to emulate these qualities. Fear of pity, rejection, and missing opportunities, however, pushed me to keep my distance and my secrets. Insecurity born from childhood pain drove me to overwork and overcompensate.

I had remained blind to the fact that my secrecy was holding me back until I hit the roadblock at TD Ameritrade. I needed to build trust with my new leadership peers, and it just wasn't happening. Another great leader, Tim Hockey, arranged for me to receive feedback from these peers.

In terms of how I liked to think of myself, the feedback hurt. It also served as a wakeup call. My decision to tell Tim about my CMT was a turning point. Taking his advice to tell my peers and my own leadership team was a radical step for me.

Michelle's question about the focus on my ALI social impact project was my final wakeup call and my fork in the road. It's fitting that the call came from Michelle, whose wisdom, insight, and support have meant so much to me at every stage of our life together.

The decision to get involved in raising funds to research a cure for CMT has changed the trajectory of my life and work. I'm an old hand at fundraising, but the first few times I talked about my CMT in front of people I'd known and worked with were scary. However, the personal and financial support I've received is nothing short of phenomenal. Whatever comes next in my career, my efforts to support CMT research will be an important part of my life.

After years of insecurity, I can finally say I don't worry about what people think of me. I have CMT. If I miss an opportunity because someone assumes I'm not up to the task, there will be other opportunities. As Michelle said to me so long ago, the disease is something I have. It's not who I am. I am a husband, father, brother, uncle, community advocate, and leader who has learned that vulnerability is a vital component of leadership strength. These are the dominant dimensions of my ever-evolving mosaic.

I'd always intended to include the concept of the mosaic in the book, but I hadn't fully realized the role it would play within my own mind as the book unfolded. I initially thought of my mosaic as a series of experiences and people, and I wrote about them in relation to jobs and experiences with a factual and objective eye.

Somewhere in the later drafts, more personal and transformative experiences began to insert themselves into the narrative. The jagged shards from my mosaic pushed themselves into the narrative alongside the smoother, more polished ones.

For example, I had expected to mention that I had CMT, but I never intended to describe the various events along that line in my mosaic, let alone share my vulnerabilities surrounding it.

The story of the obstacle course with the leadership team at TD Ameritrade was nowhere in the initial drafts. When I began the book, I was entering Harvard with the intent of doing an economic social impact project in Massachusetts. My deeper secrets were safe.

Reviewing my early pages, I see that my fear of vulnerability was itself the thing that was holding me back. As I review my final pages, I see that I am more whole, a better person and a better leader. I feel energized and ready for what comes next. Of course, that doesn't mean I'm complacent or done. I may be whole, but I'm not complete.

If I've learned anything during the season in which I wrote this book, it's that I still have plenty to learn, plenty of room to grow, and plenty left to contribute to society. An old saying goes, "There is no future in the past." While I shall look to the past for guidance, lessons, wisdom, and pride, I will be looking to the future for inspiration on what's next. Stay tuned.

Afterword

I've spent a great deal of time formulating and refining the ten leadership principles featured in this book. At the same time, I've struggled to find the right "umbrella" for a comprehensive definition of leadership. I've searched for the words that perfectly sum up the essence of leadership.

What definition captures the academic, social, relational, and personal attributes of leadership? Is leadership a science or an art? Are leaders made or born? Can leadership be taught or learned? Is leadership situational or does one pursue a similiar leadership approach in different situations?

There are literally thousands of books on the subject of leadership, each with its own nuanced ideas on the subject. Many leading philosophers and thinkers have come up with their own definitions. Here are a few to ponder.

> "The only definition of a leader is one who has followers."
> —Peter Drucker, author, management consultant

> "Leadership is the capacity to translate vision into reality."
> —Warren Bennis, author, leadership studies scholar

> "As we look into the next century, leaders will be those who empower others."
> —Bill Gates, co-founder, Microsoft

"Leadership is influence—nothing more, nothing less."
—John Maxwell, author, speaker

"[Leadership is] working with or through others to achieve objectives."
—Dr. Paul Hersey, behavioral scientist, entrepreneur

"Leadership is a process of social influence, which maximizes the efforts of others, towards the achievement of a goal."
—Kevin Kruse, author, historian

While these definitions are helpful and instructive, they still leave me wanting a more holistic description, one that addresses the scientific, artistic, academic, relational, and social dimensions. I found what I was looking for in what seemed at first to be an unlikely place.

The ceremony in which my lifelong love Michelle and I were married contained several Bible readings to help us to fully comprehend our commitment on that cold and snowy December day. One of the readings was from the First Letter of Paul to the Corinthians. Chances are you have heard it before.

Given that Paul's words in this passage are about love, it is one of the most frequently read passages at Christian weddings. It speaks to how the unbreakable bond of love can unite two people together. It speaks about respect, honor, integrity, trust, perseverance, and how to care for one another.

Paul is not referring specifically to marriage in this passage. He is writing about love as the energy of all life, the underpinning of every relationship including marriage, family, friendships, and other relationships. That reading had a powerful impact on me then and every time I have heard it since. Across the years, I often harkened back to this passage for guidance in my marriage and other relationships, personal and professional. I even began to wonder whether the principles around love enumerated in this passage might apply to leadership as well.

The complete passage is in the New Testament, Chapter 13. Given the various New Testament translations that appear in different versions of the

Holy Bible, I will offer two here. One from the New International Version (NIV), and one from the New Revised Standard Version (NRSV).

New International Version (NIV)

Love is patient, love is kind. It does not envy, it does not boast, it is not proud. It does not dishonor others, it is not self-seeking, it is not easily angered, it keeps no records of wrongs. Love does not delight in evil but rejoices with the truth. It always protects, always trusts, always hopes, always perseveres. Love never fails.

New Revised Standard Version (NRSV)

Love is patient; love is kind; love is not envious or boastful or arrogant or rude. It does not insist on its own way; it is not irritable or resentful; it does not rejoice in wrongdoing, but rejoices in the truth. It bears all things, believes all things, hopes all things, endures all things. Love never ends.

These are poetic and beautiful words about relationships. Do they have anything to say about leadership? Love isn't leadership, is it? And leadership isn't love, or is it? Maybe to be successful, leadership takes love, and love takes leadership.

I pondered on this idea for some time before a question intrigued me one day. What would happen if I substituted the word *leadership* for the words *love* and *it* in the above passages? Would I gain any insights into the true and enduring meaning of leadership? Here's how the New Revised Standard Version (NRSV) reads with the substitutions.

> *Leadership* is patient; *leadership* is kind; *leadership* is not envious or boastful or arrogant or rude. *Leadership* does not insist on its own way; *leadership* is not irritable or resentful; *leadership* does not rejoice in wrongdoing, but rejoices in the truth. *Leadership* bears all things, believes all things, hopes all things, endures all things. *Leadership* never ends.

I remember the first time I changed the words and read the revised passage. I was working as president and COO of UMB Financial Corporation. The result struck me like a lightning bolt. I read the passage to myself repeatedly. I was startled. I had finally found a leadership definition that spoke directly to me.

While this leadership definition may not speak to everyone, it spoke directly to me. This was not because the definition had Christian origins. The definition, in my view, transcends religion. It has universal application. It is about a form and style of leadership that I was completely comfortable with. It was inspirational and aspirational.

I stared at my computer screen for a long time that afternoon, trying to find fault with the words and their relevance to leadership. I challenged myself repeatedly, but I could not find fault. In my estimation it was just about perfect. It encapsulated what I believed, and how I had tried to lead throughout my career. The passage embodied everything I considered when I thought about strong, caring, moral, inspirational leaders.

As I reflected further, I knew that I fell short of this definition in many ways. There were times when I might have been knowingly or unknowingly arrogant or rude. There were certainly times when my patience wore thin as I tried to get something done. At other times, I might have taken pleasure in someone coming up short so that I might advance.

I began to feel as if this definition was unattainable, unrealistic. However, I soon recognized that it was okay to fall short of this definition. The attainment of all that this definition presented would be a never-ending journey and a continuous driver for improvement.

To me, this passage embodies the qualities of a true servant leader, one who helps others succeed and grow by removing obstacles that inhibit their success. This is a leader who puts the needs of others ahead of his or her own, one who is willing to sacrifice self for the good of the whole. Of course, it's far more popular to think that followers are obligated to sacrifice for the leader. That is not what the passage, and arguably leadership, requires.

One day I thought about sharing this significant insight with my UMB leadership team. As I was about to do so, I became concerned that some might bristle at the suggestion that the definition of leadership could be found in the Christian Bible. I certainly did not want to offend anyone. I did not want to impose my views onto them.

Ultimately, I did share this definition with my team at that time and with others over the years. I always do so with some hesitation, knowing that some will react negatively, and some will think I am out of line. Some don't believe that anything with religious tones should be discussed in business or public forums. When I do share this definition, I do so in the context of also listening and respecting differing perspectives. I've appreciated some meaningful discussions on that score.

I have struggled about whether to include this leadership definition in this book. Obviously, I decided to include it. The primary reason is that this definition is authentic to me. I've held it as my highest standard and aspiration for decades. To withhold it would be approaching dishonesty. I'm not willing to do that.

I share this passage and my interpretation of it with humility and ask that you receive it in the same way. Whether you wholeheartedly agree or not, I trust you will find some value as I share important points in the passage that, in my view, speak to its collective wisdom and power.

Leadership is patient.

According to the *Oxford English Dictionary*, patience is "the capacity to accept or tolerate delay, trouble or suffering without getting angry or upset." In my personal leadership practice, I have come to appreciate that it takes *patience* and *persistence* to accomplish big things.

My mother used to tell me I had the patience of Job, a biblical figure who suffered mightily over an excessively long period of time without wavering or wandering in his faith. Having the patience of Job, in essence, means to have a great deal of patience and faith during times of trouble and difficulty.

I have come to appreciate that strong, confident leaders have the patience to seek out and fully consider other points of view. They readily receive input from all perspectives and take enough time to absorb what others are saying. They are intentional about taking the time to listen, hear, and consider all perspectives.

Leaders who display patience are not necessarily slow to make decisions or prone to waffling. Quite to the contrary, patience is a discipline of taking in all relevant and important inputs from all sources and giving due consideration to these different perspectives when making important decisions.

It is also useful to be patient as sometimes conditions change, requiring new inputs before deciding. An old carpentry adage recommends to measure twice and cut once. That sure makes sense to me.

It's important not to confuse patience with softness. Being patient does not mean that you are easily manipulated. It doesn't mean you lack the courage to make tough decisions or hold people accountable for poor performance. It just means that you take the appropriate amount of time and conduct the due diligence to assemble and assimilate all the required facts prior to making important decisions.

Leadership is kind.

Kindness and humility are the two of most underrated and underappreciated elements of strong leadership. Kindness is defined as the quality of being friendly, generous, and considerate. Who would not want to work with a leader who embodies these characteristics? Kindness and gentleness are powerful, disarming forces—especially in times of conflict.

I once worked for a leader who was unkind to others and seemingly took delight in putting others down in public settings. Enlightened leaders understand that you do not raise yourself up by putting others down. You pull yourself down with everyone else, making it impossible to accomplish great things.

Another word for kindness is considerateness. Consideration overlaps with patience in leaders who take the time to listen to others. They consider other points of view and will often incorporate different perspectives into their final directions. In the process, they are respectful of other people's feelings.

In contrast are leaders who lead by fear. These leaders are generally insecure in some way. There is a big difference between achieving compliance and commitment. Leaders who operate through fear can achieve near-term compliance with their orders, but they will never achieve full commitment from their teams. While compliance may get good results in the short term, it takes commitment from individuals to remain fully engaged over the longer term. As for me, I will offer kindness to achieve true commitment over the use of fear to achieve compliance every day of the week.

Leadership is not envious or boastful or arrogant or rude.

Envy, along with pride, greed, lust, gluttony, wrath, and sloth make up the seven deadly sins. They are behaviors or feelings that inspire further sin. It is not easy for a leader to avoid envy. I have certainly been guilty of envying competitors who have had more or better resources, a better brand, or better technology. I have also been envious of others around me who have enjoyed a higher level of success than I might have at a given point in time.

We all know leaders who boast about their accomplishments. Sometimes they fail to mention that it was the team that achieved the results, not them individually. I have been guilty of this from time to time, especially early in my career as I was seeking to climb the corporate ladder. It took a lot of maturation on my part to realize that shining the spotlight on others does not put you in shade. Quite to the contrary: It allows the light to reflect back even brighter on you.

The need for affirmation is a natural, human need. However, focusing too much on affirmation and recognition can lead a person to be boastful, arrogant, or rude in ways that can be unbecoming in a true leader. Whenever

I have caught myself boasting about something, it has typically been to cover up some insecurity I had.

If you find yourself too often saying, "I did this" or "I did that," it might be good to check if your ego is getting in the way of allowing others to shine brightly.

Leadership does not insist on its own way.

Most leaders are in leadership positions because *someone else* believes that they possess the proper set of characteristics that enable them to lead others to levels of performance higher than if someone else were the leader. This idea of appointed leadership can make it easy for leaders to become confident (sometimes overly confident) in their own abilities. This can cause leaders to stop listening to and seeking out advice from others. This often leads to becoming closed to new ideas and ways of looking at complex multifaceted matters.

The best leaders do not insist on things being done their way. They certainly have their own well-informed point of view, but they remain open to and objective about additional solicited and unsolicited input. They seek out the *best* decisions or outcomes, not those that only mirror their already established preferred path. They focus on establishing facts and data, not just intuition and emotion to make critical decisions. I am fond of asking, "What are the incontrovertible facts?" Intuition and emotion, while helpful, are best utilized once the base of available facts, circumstances, and risks has been fully understood. An old adage goes, a well-defined problem is already half answered. Taking the time to understand the problem and to establish a reliable fact base is time well spent.

We all know leaders who will only follow the path that they prescribe, regardless of what the facts and circumstances tell them. These leaders often surround themselves with a small circle of like-minded advisors who have the preordained answer to every question. Great leaders resist this approach and always remain open to the input and wisdom of others.

Leadership is not irritable or resentful.

Irritability is the tendency to be easily annoyed or made angry. Plenty of situations give rise to irritability. Things big and small go wrong on a daily basis.

When I have been irritable, which is a natural human response to difficult situations, I have tried not to let that irritability show through to those around me. I have tried not to wear my emotions on my sleeve for others to see and interpret. That doesn't help anyone.

Our moods, words, and actions affect others. Leaders are responsible for managing their moods in the same way they are responsible for managing their time and energy. When we allow a bad day or being upset to spill over into our behavior, our teams and those we encounter can feel it. Suddenly, the entire organization is having a bad day and becomes irritable, making it difficult to get things done.

The other concept in this part of the passage is resentfulness. Resentful people hold on to grudges. A grudge causes damage in working relationships and teams. It is important to try to move past these issues—for the good of the organization, the individuals, and the teams that are counting on you. Skillful leaders know that it's impossible to fully collaborate while holding a grudge. They build mechanisms to address and resolve conflict in constructive ways.

Leadership does not rejoice in wrongdoing but rejoices in the truth.

When it comes to the political and cultural aspects of organizations, wrong and unjust things will inevitably happen. Some people will be promoted unfairly over others. Some departments will get more resources than they deserve or can effectively utilize. Some leaders will compete with rather than cooperate with other departments.

For matters under their control, true leaders seek to make ethical as well as productive decisions. For issues not under their control, they seek to influence decisions with the same guiding principles. For illegal or abusive actions, they take appropriate action. Beyond these responses, they don't spend time and energy on issues of wrongdoing. They spend energy and celebrate in uncovering truth. Truth is grounded in the establishment of proper facts and data against which outcomes can be adjudicated. In the business world the establishment of truth is essential for good decision making. In our era of fake news and lightly governed social media, it can be hard to discern truth from fiction. Establishing incontrovertible truths is more important than ever.

Leadership bears all things, believes all things, hopes all things, endures all things.

Let's face it, being a leader is difficult, a constant challenge. I watch with amazement leaders who can shoulder the innumerable burdens they face, keep a good attitude, and endure through many trials and tribulations. Think of Abraham Lincoln, who led a divided country through a brutal four-year civil war; or Franklin D. Roosevelt, who had the responsibility to lead a nation and a world after the US entered World War II; or George W. Bush, who had to lead a nation after September 11. Think of Indira Gandhi, the former prime minister of India, or Golda Meir, the former prime minister of Israel. Each of these leaders had to bear tremendous burdens, maintain an unshakable belief in the righteousness of their cause, and work to convince others of their viewpoints.

I take some exception with *leadership hopes all things*. You've heard me say that hope is not a strategy. You've also heard me say that having a clear, unambiguous strategy gives one hope. In my view, hope without a plan is wishful thinking. This is not in conflict with having faith. Faith is a strong belief in God, the doctrines of religion, or the good in the universe. It is based on a spiritual foundation rather than proof.

Leadership never ends.

It is easy to think about leadership only in the context of the workday and the workplace. After all, isn't that where the real craft of leadership is practiced?

I proffer that leadership does not end when a leader walks out the front office door or leaves the last Zoom call of the day. Leadership by necessity transcends time and place. A leader can't turn leadership on and off like a light switch. It always needs to be on.

This is something I came to understand when I was at UMB. There was no space between my professional and personal life. Whether I was inside running the organization, outside in the community, or even spending time with friends and family, I always had to be "on." It was tiring, but it comes with the territory.

Consider the business leader who attends his or her child's school basketball game and creates a scene by berating the game's referee after a contested call. Reports of that behavior will get back to the office, sullying the leader's reputation. Or consider Theranos founder Elizabeth Holmes, who carefully curated an image of herself in the model of Apple's Steve Jobs, even dressing like him, only to be exposed later as a fraud.

Leadership is a responsibility, a privilege, and a high calling. Leadership is not for the self-centered or the faint-hearted. It is not for the proud, nor for those who intentionally spew hate. Leadership is for the optimists, the ones who design and create the future. As Shimon Peres, the former Israeli prime minister, once said, "Always be optimistic, but never be satisfied." These are words to live by.

According to the definition I hold, we are all called to be leaders in an aspirational way. Some of us will find ourselves leaders in a C-suite while others will occupy a leadership role more like that of Mother Teresa. All of us will be leaders or co-leaders in a family, neighborhood, and/or a country. According to the definition in 1 Corinthians 13, I know that I fall short as a leader on a regular basis. I'm guessing you do as well. Still, I'm not discouraged. Rather, I'm inspired.

Won't you join me in the quest to fulfill the ultimate definition of leadership?

About the Author

Peter de Silva is a seasoned chairman, CEO, president, executive committee member, board director, and trustee for nonprofit organizations and national charitable foundations. de Silva is a former senior Fellow in the Advanced Leadership Initiative (ALI) at Harvard University.

With thirty-plus years in leadership, Peter is recognized for his ability to drive outsized results by creating a compelling purpose and vision, building enterprise strategies, aligning resources, and executing plans. He is a high-energy, highly engaged servant-leader who is committed to developing world-class talent and successful organizations.

Beginning in 2021, as a Fellow in the ALI, Peter spent eighteen months utilizing his deep leadership skills and passion for service to advance global social impact initiatives. He was elected by his cohort to become a member of the ALI Coalition Advisory Committee, of which he is still a member.

Peter's career includes financial services experience in all facets of banking, wealth management, trading, investments, institutional asset management, asset servicing, retirement, retail and institutional brokerage, technology, and related corporate services.

As former president of TD Ameritrade's retail business, Peter's span of responsibility was the strategic direction and support to more than nine million retail investors with more than $650 billion in client assets. He led all facets of the retail business, including strategy; branches and sales; investor services; business analytics; client experience; digitization; product development; and partnerships.

de Silva led these groups through the successful integration of Scottrade Financial Services, including the conversion of $200 billion in client assets and 3.9 million client accounts to TD Ameritrade following the company's acquisition in September 2017.

Peter served on TD Ameritrade's executive team, which shaped the strategic focus and direction of the organization. Peter was a member of the leadership team that subsequently sold TD Ameritrade to Charles Schwab.

Prior to joining TD Ameritrade, de Silva led the retail and institutional divisions for Scottrade Financial Services and served on the company's board and executive leadership team. Before joining Scottrade in 2016, he was the president and chief operating officer of UMB Financial Corporation from 2004 to 2015, and chairman and CEO of UMB Bank from 2004 to 2012. From 1987 to 2004, de Silva worked as an executive at Fidelity Investments, where he served in several leadership positions, including senior vice president/general manager of Fidelity Retail, and senior vice president of Fidelity Brokerage Company.

Peter's prior board service includes the Greater Kansas City Chamber of Commerce (board chair); the United Way of Greater Kansas City (campaign committee chair, Tocqueville Society chair); Park University; the Kansas City Symphony; the Civic Council of Greater Kansas City; the St. Louis Regional Business Council; and Kansas City Public Television (KCPT). Peter also served on the mayoral transition committee for Kansas City Mayor Sylvester James.

Peter currently serves on the boards of IRALOGIX; Edelman Financial Engines; Infosel; Onepak; Prosper Marketplace; Fidelity Security Life Insurance; and Fidelity Security Assurance Company.

Peter also currently serves on the nonprofit boards of the CMT Research Foundation; the National WWI Museum and Memorial; MRIGlobal; UMass Dartmouth Foundation; the Commonwealth Corporation; and the Robert W. Plaster Foundation.

Peter and Michelle de Silva have been married for more than thirty years. They have two grown daughters, Christine and Sarah. Peter's hobbies include cycling, boating, history, travel, fishing, reading, and leadership.

A Special Bonus from Peter

Accomplished leaders know that it takes deliberate, focused, and constant action to develop and refine their leadership skills. It is a process, not an event. Taking the time to learn and use the principles I've shared in *Taking Stock* can change the arc of your life and your career.

As you know, growth and change do not come from reading or even studying information; growth is the natural outcome of *applying* what we learn. The application of my time- and battle-tested life and leadership principles will enable you to accelerate your personal and professional development.

To help you further on this journey, I have created a downloadable Life and Leadership Principles Guide, which includes the ten principles along with key questions to consider as you implement and apply the learnings from the book. This guide will allow quick, easy, and discrete access any time you need the principles. Refer to this guide when you are looking for reinforcement that you are on the right track, need new or different perspectives to consider, or are seeking confirmation of your decisions prior to taking action.

Go to **https://PeterJdeSilva.com/gift** and tell me where to send your bonus gift.

Your contact information will never be shared, and you can unsubscribe at any time.

I'm in your corner. Let me know if I can help further.

Best,

Made in the USA
Columbia, SC
01 April 2023

dfd87936-a1c9-4c19-8911-a972deac5469R01